The

MW00770259

"Get ready to have your faith unleashed! *The Whole Story* by Meredith Perryman is just that—a complete look at God's epic story. Even if you've been a Jesus follower for years, I think you'll be surprised by the insights Meredith offers in this book as she challenges you to explore what too many of our Sunday school classes leave out in the retelling of the gospel. If you've ever wondered what difference knowing Jesus makes when your world seems dark and you feel broken, I get it. I've been there too. But what you'll discover in this book is that hope is right here, right now, today. If you're hungry for a faith that's vibrant, authentic, and full of purpose, you need to know the whole story."
—**Lauren Lucille Vasser**, stand-up comedian, speaker, and producer of The Unknown Tour

"My heart leaps for joy at the clear, concise, and powerfully transformative articulation of the gospel that Meredith Perryman shares in *The Whole Story*. This book is steeped in love and was birthed from God and Meredith's beloved relationship—a relationship He desires to have with all humanity. *The Whole Story* is a beautifully crafted tool for followers of Christ who want to better understand our *raison d'etre* and God's big-picture calling on each believer's life. At the same time, this book communicates to those who have not yet seen and embraced God's everlasting love for them manifested in Jesus, God's Christ. I will use this book again and again to both ends."
—**Jennifer Rousseau Cumberbatch**, founder and leader of Full Measure

"Always the teacher, Meredith takes us on a great journey from her own vulnerability to a place of discovery. Meredith's ability to break down 'the whole story' and show all God has for each of us challenges you and me to live in light of the full gospel. And as we truly live, Meredith reminds us of our hope in Christ and the power that hope gives us to 'shine God's light to expand His kingdom.' We live in a world filled with darkness. But, as Scripture reminds us, Jesus has overcome the world. As we search for what can be done, what I can do (broken as I am), Meredith reminds us of God's relentless pursuit of relationship with us and provides comfort that emboldens us to relentlessly love others. I know you will enjoy this book. I am excited about all you will receive through Meredith's words. I am expectant of what God has for you and for me, as we embrace the whole story."

—**Kyle Salmon**, executive director of
Save our Streets Ministries

"My dear friend Meredith Perryman's book *The Whole Story* is a powerful exploration of what it truly means to live unhindered in the light of the gospel. She reminds us of the profound freedom we have in Christ and points us to the purpose and calling God has for our lives so we can break free from the prisons we tend to find ourselves in—prisons of shame, doubt, and loss. Meredith lives what she writes! We were never meant to live in these prisons; we were created for more. Meredith's relatable stories and well-researched insights in *The Whole Story* will inspire you, and most importantly, direct you to God's truths to fulfill your deepest longings."

—**Marian Jordan Ellis**, Christian speaker and Bible study
author of *For His Glory* and *Behold and Believe*

"Meredith is the real deal. *The Whole Story* is the fruit of years of diligently studying and teaching God's word, walking through pain and loss, and wrestling with God and not letting go. The words Meredith shares were hard fought for and are a blessing to her and to us—her readers.

"I trust this book will challenge you, cause you to look at God's story with fresh perspective, and deeply encourage you to walk more closely and freely with Jesus. That is what reading *The Whole Story* has done for me."

—**Jamie Suel**, director of missionary care and development at Vianations.org

"Meredith Perryman's *The Whole Story* feels like a chat with your wise friend who's been through it all. Her openness about her own struggles and spiritual growth gives you the hope that comes with knowing you aren't alone. This book isn't about lofty ideals; it's about how to live your faith every day. Meredith's advice on being grounded in Scripture, soaking up God's love, and connecting with others is practical and down-to-earth. *The Whole Story* is a reminder that faith isn't about perfection; it's about embracing freedom and purpose. Meredith's relatable insights and empowering words make this book a must-read for anyone who desires to grow in their faith journey."

—**Christine Wolf Hoover**, MA, LPC, NCC, trauma-informed psychotherapist and Christian speaker

"I've never heard *The Whole Story* articulated so clearly, with the Father's heart for His earthly creation motivating every heavenly move. His longing to be with us started in Genesis and has not lost momentum. And the beauty of Jesus being heaven on earth in us is mind-blowing. Meredith started teaching this years ago, and I'm so very grateful it made it to the written page, with God's Word anchoring every chapter."

—**Leah Sequeira**, founder of Breakthrough to Purpose Life & Leadership Coaching

"In studying the Hebrew roots of my faith in Jesus, I have come to appreciate so much . . . the depth and layers of how Meredith fleshes out historical and cultural context from antiquity. Details can change everything! I believe the Holy Spirit has guided her to share rich details that add deeper understanding. I could not put it down!"

—**Debbie Benaglio**, certified life coach and
founder of inKind, Inc.

"There are times when you begin reading a book and everything that you are experiencing is articulated on the pages for you to unravel for yourself. From the first chapters of this book, Meredith brings light and hope to the reader. We don't have to settle or accept the status quo but can live beyond our fears, hurts, and past trauma. Meredith made a decision to be vulnerable in her writing in a relatable way, and it paid off.

"Thank you, Meredith, for reminding us of biblical truth and building us up amidst trauma. We were made for more, and I'm determined to live the full gospel, rooted in His love."

—**Michelle A. Thomas**, believer, author,
speaker, and podcaster

THE WHOLE STORY

Eternity from the Beginning

Meredith Perryman

The Whole Story
© 2023 by Meredith Perryman

This book is available at special discounts when purchased in quantity for use as premiums, promotions, fundraisers, or for educational purposes. For inquiries, visit meredithperryman.com/contact.

Published by Courageous Heart Press
College Station, Texas
In partnership with
THE *FREEONE*

Editing and Design by My Writers' Connection
Title Illustration by McKenna Ryan
Figures by Angela Robinson

Library of Congress Control Number: 2023947272

Hardback ISBN: 978-1-950714-30-8
Paperback ISBN: 978-1-950714-29-2
Ebook ISBN: 978-1-950714-31-5

First Printing: October 2023

CONTENTS

For Sibyl Slocomb, my grandmother, whom we affectionately called Mom-Mom.
Thank you for sowing faithful prayers all your life.
You are greatly missed, but your legacy remains strong.

Foreword

Do you know that feeling of surprised delight that comes when you put on a new pair of eyeglasses for the first time? Suddenly, you can see things you didn't even realize were there before. Or maybe you remember seeing an old black-and-white movie that had been updated in Technicolor and saw the story come to life in new and colorful ways. As you encounter the message in the pages ahead, I believe a similar kind of experience is available to you.

More than twenty years after Jesus radically changed my life, I heard Meredith deliver this message. I thought I already saw in color, but as I began to see in a new way through the lens of the full gospel—*the whole story*—everything became more vibrant. As a follower of Jesus, and as someone who desires to live on mission, I can honestly say that the truth revealed in *The Whole Story* has absolutely and radically transformed the ways I think, live, and lead. The more I read and learn from Meredith, the more I understand God's plan to restore and expand His kingdom in us and throughout the earth.

I have had the privilege of partnering together with Meredith as she teaches thousands of men and women in various settings. Each time, I learn something new and feel blessed to watch people's amazing *ah-ha* moments as they see the gospel in new ways for themselves.

My prayer is that as you read *The Whole Story*, you, too, will be able to see and experience the gospel in a way that is fuller and more vibrant than you've previously understood it to be. I encourage you to read this book again and again. Underline passages that surprise and perhaps challenge you to think differently about God's story and His plan for you. Tag pages for future reference. Share what you discover. Above all, allow the Holy Spirit to use this book and God's Word to change you. As it has for me, I pray this message releases you in a new way to be a part of God's heart of Restoration.

Stephanie Lee
Founder and Director of You Are, Inc.
youareconference.com

Author's Note

During a challenging season of life, when I began to question the goodness of God and the gospel, I turned to the living and breathing Word of God for truth and clarity. I also sought out the teachings and inspiration from giants in the faith who have gone before me. In writing this book, I am humbly standing on their shoulders.

I am not a Bible scholar. Instead, what I am is a grateful student on a journey of learning. Contained in these pages is a compilation of what I learned from scholars, teachers, and authors during my time of searching and questioning. Some of their teachings have become so ingrained in me that, honestly, where their words end and mine begin has become a bit fuzzy. It's my desire, however, to give credit where it is due. To the best of my ability, I have searched for and noted original sources. Sincere apologies for anything I have missed.

Chapter 1

Hindered

Therefore, since we are surrounded by such a great cloud of witnesses, let us throw off everything that hinders and the sin that so easily entangles. And let us run with perseverance the race marked out for us, fixing our eyes on Jesus, the pioneer and perfecter of faith.
—Hebrews 12:1–2a, NIV

My life rested on a stool supported by four sturdy legs. They upheld my life securely enough that I barely paid them any mind—until each one came crashing down.

At thirty-eight, and having attended church most of my life, I considered myself to be a seasoned believer. For well over a decade, I had been a Bible study participant, even a Bible teacher. I had attended countless conferences, read tons of devotional and theology books, and participated in various small groups for years. You know, seasoned:

Seasoned — see'zund (adj): I'm a grown-up and don't have to be in church but choose to be. I can tell you a few things I believe the Bible says with confidence; I raise my hands when I worship; I pray out loud in groups, etc.

I felt secure, as if nothing could throw my walk with God significantly off course. Then, one by one, the things I thought were solid, crumbled. The four legs of my life's stool gave way and sent me crashing into a dark and lonely place.

The first leg of my stool to fall was my church family. Having moved from Houston after starting a family, God led us to a church we loved in our new hometown. We rooted ourselves there deeply. My husband and I participated in an Adult Bible Fellowship class, and we eventually taught and served in different ministry areas.

This church had been our home for seven years when an ugly division tore it apart. Surprisingly, it wasn't a scandal that caused the damage, but disagreements and misunderstandings. A sad, rapid escalation of disunity ensued. Within three months, the church fired two pastors. Three others resigned. During that time, I witnessed betrayal and slander that never would have been permissible in a secular work environment. The painful ordeal shattered my trust as I experienced firsthand that churches aren't always places of ministry and healing. Sometimes, regretfully, they are places of abuse and anguish.

The next leg to give way was my marriage. My husband began traveling for work and was home only a few days a month. *A few days a month!* (Mad props to military families and single moms and dads!) We had always been a team, but I suddenly felt very much on my own. While I spent my days and nights at home with four young children, he sent me selfies from Australia. It seemed my phone would *ding* right when I was in the middle of mopping up a sewage leak that had flooded our house, taking care of a kid who had vomited all night, or visiting the veterinary ER at midnight with two dogs who had gotten into a huge bag of chocolate chips. All I could think in those moments was, *no honey, I don't want to see a picture of the Sydney Opera House again or of the incredible meal you're enjoying—**that you didn't have to cook!*** My husband and I were living completely different lives. His was exciting and interesting, and mine felt lonely and utterly overwhelming.

Then the friendship leg of my stool crumbled. Out of nowhere and with no explanation, one of my core, do-life-with friendships ended. My children referred to this friend and her husband as aunt and uncle and to their kids as cousins. We went from talking every day and regularly getting our families together to having absolutely no contact. I reached out through repeated calls and texts, attempting to understand what had happened, but my friend refused to respond. The gut-wrenching loss left me and my family wondering what was going on—and why.

The last leg to fail was my identity. During this season of upheaval, my family required every moment of my life and demanded every ounce of my energy. At the end of the day, I had nothing left to give. Unable to keep up with the never-ending list of responsibilities that each day brought, I stepped down from directing and teaching the Bible study I had been involved in for almost a decade. It was the best decision for me and our family at the time; one I still do not regret, but the sudden disengagement of going from leading the Bible study to not participating in it at all left a void. I had grown accustomed to spending time with the group weekly and devoting hours to preparation. I missed having the support of that community, and I missed spending time in God's Word.

With the four legs of my stool in splinters, I experienced a tremendous loss of purpose and identity. Aside from being a mom of four and a wife to a husband who was rarely home, I didn't know who I was. I questioned my value as a person, my worth in the community, and my place in the church. All the while, life for everyone else seemed to move along just fine without me.

Imprisoned by Lies

The depression I had fought after having children came back with a vengeance, sending me into darkness and separating me from hope.

I know now that those problems weren't unique or insurmountable. And I knew even then that they weren't comparable to the suffering many people endure. But the loss of my church family and a dear friendship, the long-distance disintegration of my marriage, and feeling a profound lack of purpose and identity—all at the same time—sent me tumbling into a desperate place.

Imprisoned by my thoughts and circumstances, I felt lonely and emotionally bruised. But I wasn't completely alone. Circling the bars of my prison was someone who knew exactly what to do with my pain and confusion: Satan.

Our enemy doesn't have any problem kicking us when we're down. He actively searches for opportunities to deceive and isolate us—all to separate us from God and His community.

Satan taunted me with doubts. Although I couldn't see him, I could hear his relentless and brutal lies.

You can't trust or count on the church.

Your heart isn't safe with them. Neither is your family.

You thought you had a great marriage, didn't you? But really, you can't count on anyone but yourself.

You took a chance and opened up your heart to a friend, but when she got to know the real you, she saw that you are not worth knowing and not worth fighting for.

You don't bring much to the table. She knows it. Everyone knows it.

You are a nobody and unworthy of being loved. God doesn't want you, and neither does anyone else.

You do not belong, and you never will.

You cannot trust God with your life or with your heart. God won't protect you.

Satan just wouldn't stop! The deception continued until it was all I could hear. Before I realized what was happening, I accepted his words as truth. One by one, each lie became another bar in the prison that surrounded me.

Even in the darkness, I never doubted the reality of God.

I did, however, doubt His goodness.

I loved God, but I didn't like him very much because I felt betrayed and rejected by Him.

Disillusioned and weary, I went through the motions of study and worship, but inside I felt dead and cynical. So cynical, in fact, when others would sincerely say (about someone who wasn't a Christian), "That person needs Jesus," all I could think was, *why? How does having Jesus help you in* this *life? How does Jesus make* this *life better?*

I mean, I *had* Jesus. But having Him didn't take away the ache of loss and loneliness. And it sure didn't prevent hardships or betrayals.

Trapped by depression, brokenness, and pain, I clung to the hope that someday I would leave this earth to live with Jesus. Only then would I be truly and forever free.

Crying Out from the Darkness

Deep down, I knew something had to be wrong with my way of thinking. I knew, too, that I didn't want to live my life cowering in a cage like a victim, while my conquered enemy whispered lies in my ear. Was I going to let Satan win? Was I going to walk away from God?

In desperation, I cried out to God. Day after day, for *months*, I offered the same plea: "God! Isn't the gospel supposed to be good news? I know it is! Show me how it is good news for *right now*, today, in *this* life! Wake up this dead and cynical part of my heart!"

And He did.

Holding onto the promise, "Draw near to God, and He will draw near to you,"* I dug into the Word. I

---

*   James 4:8 (ESV)

gathered with trusted friends and wept and confessed what I was going through. I read books and listened to different teachings on the gospel, my identity, and the goodness of God. I learned more about the Holy Spirit. I found a coach and mentor to walk with me through this journey.

---

*You can live unhindered– free–in the life God has in store for you **today**.*

Change didn't happen overnight, but I gained clarity with each step I took.

With my passion for the truth of God reignited, the darkness lifted. As it did, I saw that the door to the prison that held me wasn't locked. It never had been. Tentatively, I pushed back against the lies. As the heavy door swung open, God's light filtered in and offered a kind of freedom I craved but never dared to expect on this side of Heaven.

For the first time in my life, I experienced what it felt like to live *unhindered* by the weight of expectations and demands I had carried for so long.

Are you ready to live *unhindered?*

Perhaps you picked up this book because you feel, as I did, trapped by your circumstances, weighed down by disappointment, hurt by the church, friends, and even family members, and lost in your own life. The door to the prison of stress, fatigue, discouragement, or anxiety that surrounds you may appear to be securely locked—and that breaking free of the overwhelming *shoulds* and *musts* running your life is going to take a lot more than a nail file—or even a sledgehammer.

Doubts, fears, and challenges may have you asking questions like those I asked: *Is this all there is? Is this the best God has to offer? Is the gospel really good news for today, or is it only about life after death?*

Or maybe you are in (or anticipating) a season of transition or loss from:

- single to married,
- childlessness to motherhood,
- motherhood to childlessness,
- full-time mom to an empty nester,
- married to divorced or widowed,
- a 24/7 caregiver to suddenly alone,
- leader to feeling abandoned or unnecessary, or
- from employed to retired or fired.

Major life changes, even when they are what you wanted and prayed for, can cause you to question who you are and how or *if* you fit into the world around you.

Perhaps you've wondered lately, *who am I if I'm no longer a mom, daughter, employee, leader, _____? Does my life matter? Do I matter?*

My sweet friend, I want you to know with unwavering certainty that the door to any spiritual or emotional prison holding you is not locked. You can live unhindered—*free*—in the life God has in store for you *today*. Yes, Heaven awaits, but in the meantime, God offers you His goodness *right now*. You have a unique identity in His kingdom, and it has nothing to do with what you do but Whose you are.

And, yes, I understand that those pretty, hope-filled words may sound like platitudes—easy to say but without much substance. I understand that because until the door of my cage swung wide and God's light shone in, I used to think the same thing.

If you're feeling lost, discouraged, weary, or disillusioned in your faith, welcome. You are in the right place. Just as others did for me, I hope you'll allow me to walk alongside you and share with you what I've learned from God's Word so that you, too, can live *unhindered*.

Chapter 2

Hungry for More

I came that they may have life, and have it abundantly.
—John 10:10b, NRSV

Think about this for a minute: If someone were to ask you what the gospel is, how would you answer?

No, seriously. Think about it.

For the first forty years of my life, if someone asked me to explain the gospel to them, this is how I responded:

In the beginning, God created the heavens and the earth and all that is in them. He then created Adam and Eve. He placed them in a garden and told them not to eat from the tree of the knowledge of good and evil. They did not obey God. Instead, they listened to the serpent. On that day, sin and death entered the world. And now, as a result, we are all born sinners, separated from God, living in a cursed world.

That is called *the Fall*. It explains the *problem* of sin.

But here's the good news! Jesus Christ gave His life on the cross to pay for our sins. His death bridged the gap between us and a holy God. If we believe in Him, when we die, we will spend eternity with God.

This is called *Redemption*. It is God's *solution* to the problem.

If you believe that Jesus died for your sins, you, too, will be forgiven and get to live with God for eternity.

The Gospel = *Fall* and *Redemption*

The End.

Now, you may be wondering what could be wrong with that answer. It is a pretty good summation of the Romans Road and what the Bible tracts say. It covers all the colors of the beads on the salvation bracelet, right?

And you're right. There's nothing inaccurate in that summary of the gospel. On the contrary, all of it is true and vital, and all of it is good.

It is, however, *incomplete*.

The gospel is not *only* about the Fall and Redemption. Although they are key components, the Fall and Redemption only comprise part of God's story. So much more is going on in God's Word! When we consider *all* of Scripture, we discover that the good news of God is even bigger and better than the limited version many of us have trusted for years.

I didn't understand that when I became a Bible teacher fifteen-plus years ago. My passion was to teach

God's Word so that believers could live *in* the world but not *of* the world. I wanted to encourage people to tell others about Jesus, so they, too, would go to Heaven when they died. Teaching the truth as I knew it, I had unknowingly reduced the gospel to a formula for getting into Heaven.

Ask Jesus into your heart

=

go to Heaven when you die.

With that incomplete understanding of the gospel, I clung to the *going to Heaven* part. It was my hope! One day, I would die and go to Heaven and finally escape the pain and heartache caused by the sin and darkness of the world.

"Is this it, God? Is this what You died for? Is this what You are all about?"

When times were tough, I comforted myself by taking a deep breath, closing my eyes, and repeating the promise: "God is in control. Life is hard. But one day Jesus will return and set all things right, or I will die and go to live with Him until He does."

In the interim, it seemed, my only recourse amidst so much hate, depravity, and darkness was to beg Jesus to return. I believed that things were going to continue to get worse as sin increased, and all I could do was suffer through it. Well, that, and try to introduce as many people as I could to Jesus while I waited for Him to return and make things right.

Made for More

Waiting for anything is hard, especially when the expectation is that you'll be waiting your *entire life* for your hope to be fulfilled. I had done a pretty good job of hanging on to that hope, though, until my *entire life* toppled. Then suddenly, that incomplete gospel just didn't cut it for me. With splinters of loneliness, loss, and heartache festering in my heart, the version of the gospel I had relied on and taught for so long *felt* incomplete.

Because it *was*.

I remember looking around at the people who had gathered for worship on Sunday mornings and wondering, *is this really what being a believer is all about?* From the outside, we all looked fine, dressed for church, ready to sing the songs, and listen to the stories. But as we smiled and greeted one another, I wondered if anyone else felt the darkness pressing in around them. *Can anyone see the bars of my prison? Do they have their own?* Then we would go home, knowing we would repeat the process the next Sunday, and the one after that.

On the good days, I went home feeling (temporarily) uplifted.

But those were not the good days, which meant that I often felt a sense of relief when I pulled out of the church parking lot.

Sunday after Sunday, the same questions came up in my prayers: "Is this it, God? Is this what You died for? Is this what *You* are all about?"

Even later, as I buried myself in Scripture and relied on God's Word to combat Satan's lies, that discontent remained. My relationship with the Lord had deepened, but I couldn't quiet the nagging sense in my heart that the hope of Christ had to be about more than waiting for Heaven.

During this time, I grew weary of the well-intentioned platitudes some people offered as the answers to my search.

"You don't know what the future holds, but you know who holds the future."

"God always has a reason."

"When God closes a door, He opens a window."

"Let go and let God."

"God will never give you more than you can handle."

"God works in mysterious ways."

Rather than soothing me, those words frustrated me. They held no transformative power for me or the world around me. It got to the point that I thought I might throw one of my good Sunday morning shoes at the next person who told me to "abide," "walk by the Spirit," or "cease striving."

The thing is, I believed in the beautiful promises I read in God's Word. I recognized the truth in the words I sang in worship. I knew the Bible stories about people whose lives God had changed. I even personally knew a few individuals whose lives God had radically transformed with His love.

I believed the Word of God to be alive and active.

I believed that Jesus came to give us abundant life.

I believed that God is *the* all-powerful God who defeated Satan and has overcome the world.

I believed that Jesus ushered in the Kingdom of Heaven with His death and resurrection.

I believed all these truths then, and I *wanted* to believe that the gospel was good news *for today.*

So what was my problem?

My problem was the disconnect between what I believed and my reality. I knew all the words to the songs and had memorized the scriptures, but there was an undeniable chasm between the hope and freedom offered in those words and what I was experiencing in my life. My heart and spirit longed for more.

I didn't want simply to read and sing about God's promises; I wanted to *live* them. I wanted to know the reality of Jesus's peace, the Spirit's joy, and God's goodness.

If I believed, why was I struggling to see how Jesus makes *this* life better?

I didn't know the whole story.

In His mercy, God revealed to me through His Word and other books, such as N.T. Wright's *Surprised by Hope* and Scot McKnight's *The King Jesus Gospel,* that I didn't have the whole story. He had much more to offer than the gospel I had reduced to a formula for getting into Heaven.

My soul hungered for more because that's how God created me—*and you.*

He created us with purpose and offers us a calling, not *just* to spend someday with Him, but to know and experience eternity, starting now.

God promises that when we seek Him with all our hearts, we will find Him.* I searched, and God delivered by helping me understand that the gospel isn't only about the Fall (our problem) and Redemption (God's solution.) Yes, those are obviously essential parts of the story, but the *full* gospel—the whole story—has a beginning and an end that I'd been overlooking all my life: *Creation* (our calling) and *Restoration* (God's plan for all of creation).

The Full Gospel =

Creation   +   Fall   + Redemption + Restoration

The gospel I had grown up knowing and later teaching cut off the beginning and end of God's story. For years, I had missed the magnitude of God—who He is, what He has done, what He is doing, and what He is going to do!

The *full* gospel *is* for Heaven, but it also applies to our lives *right here* and *right now*.

If the Fall and Redemption sum up the gospel you've been taught, it may seem complete. Those two parts are important information, vital even, but the promise of Heaven—of someday living without sorrow or suffering—is not enough to satisfy and sustain you day-to-day when your marriage falls apart, your relationships

---

*   Jeremiah 29:13

> ## *God's story does not start with a problem. It starts with creation and a calling.*

crumble, or darkness closes in on your mind. In times like that, we need the bigger picture. We need the whole story.

What did I miss?

Imagine that someone wanted to share the Star Wars story with you for the first time. But instead of starting at the beginning, they only showed you their favorite movie in the trilogy, *The Empire Strikes Back*.

The film is the second in the Star Wars trilogy, and although your friend has told you a thousand times that "It's *fantastic*," you're having a hard time seeing the appeal. And no wonder! You'd be completely lost because you jumped into the middle of the story. *Who is this Luke and Han? What is "the force?" A princess wearing a snowsuit? What gives?* Without context, it would be difficult to understand or appreciate *The Empire Strikes Back.*

Without the resolution in *The Return of the Jedi*, you would be left wondering what happens to poor frozen Han. You wouldn't have the whole story and would probably wonder, *That's Star Wars? What's all the fuss about?*

If you don't share my love of Star Wars, just apply this scenario to any epic story or *any* story. Have you ever been sitting on the couch, watching an episode of your favorite show, when someone sat down beside you and began asking a million questions? "Who is that? What's her relationship with that guy? Why is he in prison?" If you're watching an episode in season eight, you've got a lot of backstories to cover to bring the person up to speed. If you want the person to love the show as much as you do, you know you'll have to pause and recap the highlights so they'll be able to understand what's going on. Otherwise, they'll be lost—or keep interrupting the show with more questions!

Or maybe you're the person who falls asleep during every movie. One of the first things you probably ask when the lights go up in the theater is, "What did I miss? How did the movie end?"

The bottom line is this: We need to know the whole story, from start to finish, to fully enjoy and understand it. The same thing is true for the greatest story of all, God's story—the gospel.

By focusing exclusively on the Fall and Redemption, we cut off the beginning and the end of God's story. We mistakenly limit the gospel, making it all about us and our sin and how God forgives us.

Yes, the Fall and Redemption are important—*essential*—parts of the gospel, but there's so much more to God's story than that. If we stop with the Fall and Redemption, we lack the context that gives us purpose and the hope that comes from seeing the story through to its completion. We miss the magnitude of the gospel and misunderstand our role in God's larger story, the role He empowers us to live out right here, right now.

God's story does not start with a problem. It starts with *Creation* and a *calling*.

God's story does not end with His solution to the problem of sin (as wonderful as that gift is). It ends with the *Restoration* of His original plan for each of us both now and in the age to come!

God's story, the full gospel, begins with *Creation*. So let's start at the beginning.

Creation

Chapter 3
Created for Relationship

So God created mankind in his own image, in the image of God he created them; male and female he created them.
—Genesis 1:27, NIV

And now, Father, glorify me in your presence with the glory I had with you before the world began.
—John 17:5, NIV

Do you remember the day you met your best childhood friend? Or if you're married, do you remember your first date with your future spouse?

Those moments drew you into the start of a relationship that changed your life. Even if that relationship with your friend or spouse has ended, you are different because of the time you spent together.

What about the moment you first believed Jesus loved you enough to die for you? My friends who met Jesus as adults often have a very clear memory of the day or moment that they first understood their need for a Savior. But if you're like me and you grew up going to Bible class, you may not remember the exact moment. The reality of God and the knowledge that Jesus is His son seems like it has always been part of your life. Perhaps for you, the moment you remember is the day you publicly declared your faith in Him because you understood that you needed a Savior to make it to Heaven.

Those moments are often brought on by the story of the gospel—the part that shows us our sinful, desperate state and God's saving grace. Is that story true? Absolutely. And it's a good one. It just skips over an important part of the story, the beginning.

God remembers the moment He created you, just like you might remember your best friend's birthday or your wedding anniversary. You and His relationship with you are that important to Him.

In the Beginning

In the beginning, God created the heavens and the earth.
—Genesis 1:1, ESV

Like all stories, every relationship has a beginning. Skipping the introduction to "get to the good part" can leave us confused about the story's meaning or even conflicted about its truth. That's why, when it comes to understanding the full story of the gospel, we must start at the beginning: Creation. That's where God's relationship with humanity starts—and that relationship is what shapes our existence.

As God spoke all things into existence, Scripture says He saw that His creation was *good*. Not just good, but *very good*. **Everything—the whole universe—contained God's goodness and blessing.**

This is where the gospel begins.

It's also where we meet our Creator.

In the care and imagination of creation, we see God's nature. In His design—in everything from the intricacy of the smallest creature to the complexity of the human form—we see His character. In His relationship with Adam and Eve, we see His heart. It is in this relationship that we discover God's original desire for mankind and His purpose and calling for our lives today.

> *And God saw everything that he had made, and*
> *behold, it was very good.*
> —Genesis, 1:31a, ESV

Our all-powerful Creator formed and filled the heavens and the earth and planted a garden in Eden. There, amidst the beauty of His creation, He breathed life into Adam and Eve. The gospel story I learned as a child used this *very good* beginning as a launching pad to jump straight to Genesis Chapter 3, where the problem of sin enters the story, a.k.a. the *Fall*.

But let's not be so hasty! Instead, let's examine the story of *creation* more thoroughly and consider *why* God created the world.

What does that have to do with the gospel?

Everything.

Answering the question of *why* takes us to the heart of who God is.

Why did God create?

So why did God create the world and everything in it?

The quick answer is this: God is intensely and fundamentally relational.

Read that again.

God created because He is intensely and fundamentally relational.

Lest that become another cliché we throw around without fully understanding, let's unpack what it means to be *relational*. Understanding that will help us understand God's heart for relationship with us.

Relational vs. Transactional

Imagine you're visiting with a good friend who is telling you about people she recently met at a party. Over coffee or a London Fog* (my favorite hot drink), she tells you about her new friend Latonya.

"It was easy to be around Latonya. From the moment I met her, I could tell she is a very relational person," your friend says.

Right away, you get a picture of the kind of person Latonya is. You also understand why your friend likes her so much.

The word *relational* depicts someone open and engaging, someone who comes across as sincerely inquisitive and genuinely interested in getting to know the other person. Being relational is all about creating a connection with others. Those connections deepen and eventually develop into relationships—spouses, friends, mentors, and colleagues.

You've met those people, like Latonya, who are givers. Their caring nature easily draws others into positive relationships.

You've probably also met people who are *transactional*. Opposite of relational, transactional people approach relationships from a self-centered perspective. They are takers. If they invest time in a relationship, it's because they want (and expect) something in return. Rather than operating from a sincere desire to know the other person, those who are transactional establish relationships only when there's something to be gained.

These are the kids who befriend the A+ students to get them to do their homework. They are the people who strategically choose to be friends with people who can elevate their status.

They're also the "good" Christians who work hard to obey all the rules in hopes of earning favor and love from God. (*Ouch!*) This one gets me every time because I don't *want* to have a transactional relationship with God; in reality, I can't because He is relational. God's love is unconditional. It's my nature, not His, that places a transactional value on my relationship with God.

God's love is unconditional. It's my nature, not His, that places a transactional value on my relationship with God.

Even knowing the truth of God's intense and fundamentally relational character, I have to remind myself daily that He is not transactional.

What about you? Consider the questions below and how every *yes* response affects the way you view your relationship with God:

- Do you make deals with God? *If you answer this prayer, God, I promise I will . . .*

- Do you believe that you must spend a certain number of hours or days in prayer before God will consider or answer your request?

- Do you feel God will not be with you in the same way on a day you didn't get to spend a designated amount of time with Him in prayer and in the Word?

- Do you believe you must suffer a bit before God truly forgives you for a transgression?

- Do you think God's love for you lessens when you've had an off day and haven't made the best decisions?

- Do you feel God owes you for the years you've spent volunteering in your church?

I wish I could say no to all of these, but as a work in progress, I still struggle. What a relief and reassurance to know deep down in my bones that God is *not* transactional. He is purely relational.

God created you and me, not because He wants us to try to earn His love with our performance but because it is His delight to know us. All He wants is our hearts—imperfections and all.

The God who made the world and everything in it,
being Lord of heaven and earth, does not live in temples
made by man, nor is he served by human hands, as
though he needed anything, since he himself gives to
all mankind life and breath and everything. And he
made from one man every nation of mankind to
live on all the face of the earth, having determined
allotted periods and the boundaries of their dwelling
place, **that they should seek God, and perhaps**
feel their way toward him and find him. *Yet he*
is actually not far from each one of us.
—Acts 17:24–27, ESV
(emphasis added)

God's Heart for Relationship

In the beginning God created the heavens and the
earth. Now the earth was formless and empty,
darkness was over the surface of the deep, and the
Spirit of God was hovering over the waters.
—Genesis 1:1–2, NIV

From the opening line of the creation story, we learn that
God is relational. God exists—has always existed—in
relationship. Reading Genesis 1:1, we can identify two
who were present in the very beginning when the earth
was formless and empty: God and the Spirit of God.

Was that all? Was anyone else there? We find the
answer in another account of the creation in John's Gospel:

In the beginning was the Word, and the Word was
with God, and the Word was God. He was with God
in the beginning. . . . The Word became flesh and

made his dwelling among us. We have seen his glory, the glory of the one and only Son, who came from the Father, full of grace and truth.
—John 1:1, 14, NIV

John tells us there was another presence with God in the beginning: the Word. Making it clear that the Word and God are distinct—but they are also the same—John identifies the Word as Jesus, the Son of God.

Before the foundation of the world, and before God created animals or mankind, God the Father, God the Son, and God the Holy Spirit—the Trinity—dwelt together *in relationship* with one another and as *one*.

What might it have been like between them? What did they do? At what point did they decide to create the world? These are the kinds of questions that make my brain hurt! Honestly, I have never been able to fully wrap my mind around the concept of God as three in one. For a long time, I didn't even try to understand the relationship of the Trinity. I didn't think my understanding mattered that much, as long as I believed. I know now, however, that understanding this divine

God is so intensely and fundamentally relational that, before the creation of the world, He existed in the unity of the Trinity.

relationship, which existed *before* the creation of the world, helps us understand the heart of God and His desire to create *us*.

Scripture gives us a glimpse in John 17 of the relationship between God the Father, God the Son, and God the Holy Spirit before the creation of the world. In this passage, we find Jesus, the Son of God, praying in Gethsemane. His prayer offers insight into the Trinity's relationship:

> *Father, the hour has come. Glorify your Son, that your Son may glorify you. . . . I have brought you glory on earth by finishing the work you gave me to do. And now, Father, glorify me in your presence **with the glory I had with you before the world began.***
> —John 17:1, 4–5, NIV
> (emphasis added)

> *Father, I want those you have given me to be with me where I am, and to see my glory, the glory you have given me because you loved me **before the creation of the world**. Righteous Father, though the world does not know you, I know you, and they know that you have sent me. I have made you known to them, and will continue to make you known in order that the love you have for me may be in them and that I myself may be in them.*
> —John 17:24–26, NIV
> (emphasis added)

Did you catch the phrases that give us a peek into the relationship Jesus had with the Father before the world began? These verses explain that Jesus and the Father were together *before the world existed*, glorifying and loving one another. God is so intensely and fundamentally relational that, before the creation of the world, He existed in the unity of the Trinity. God the Father, God the Son, and God the Holy Spirit glorified and loved one another in perfect relationship.

Just as it's impossible for our human minds to fully grasp the concept of God as three in one, we may not completely comprehend what that *glorifying* and *loving* one another looked (or looks) like while we're on this side of eternity. And that's okay. As the Apostle Paul wrote in 1 Corinthians 13:12 (ESV), "For now we see in a mirror dimly, but then face to face. Now I know in part; then I shall know fully, even as I have been fully known."

We don't have the capacity to see or comprehend the magnitude of God's love. Even the healthiest relationships on earth demonstrate only a fraction of God's reality.

We do, however, get glimpses of that perfection today in both fictional and real-life relationships. I can't help but think of Frodo Baggins and Samwise Gamgee's friendship in *The Lord of the Rings*, Pooh and Piglet, or Jonathan and David in Scripture. I imagine a friendship and community based on love, devotion, and intention. In such relationships, each individual is loved and valued for who they are. No one is expected to break themselves into pieces to fit in. Everyone cheers for everyone else, never feeling threatened by another's success. In these relationships, each person listens to and hears the others, and the truth is spoken in love. I imagine Jesus's words from the Sermon on the Mount* being lived out.

---

*   Matthew 5–7

An Act of Love

Where am I going with this? To the very beginning—the catalyst for creation.

If God had been alone before the creation of the world, there would be no relationship, no glorifying, no love. God's act of creation, then, would be *foremost* an execution of His will, a display of His power. As a result, the fundamental basis of reality, the thing that was before all other things, would be power.

Scripture tells a different story. God did not exist alone but in perfect unity with God the Son and God the Holy Spirit. Where there is more than one, there are relationships. And this divine relationship is characterized as one that *glorifies* and *loves* the other.

Before all things and above all things, God is love. Love is the fundamental basis—the heart—of God's creation and our reality. In other words, creation was an act of love. God created foremost not from power or will (although His power and will were certainly evidenced) but from His abundance of love and a desire to share that love.

God made Adam and Eve because He wanted an emotionally intimate relationship with them. As their Creator, God wanted them to know Him and love Him—and for them to allow Him to love them right back.

Whoever does not love does not know God, because
God is love.
—1 John 4:8, NIV

The Difference Love Makes

Growing up, I did not understand that creation was an act of love. I thought God created because He is powerful and that creation served to demonstrate His incomparable power.

I know I'm not alone in this misunderstanding. As humans, we tend to ascribe our flawed human nature to God, so we assume that power was His reason for creation. I've even heard some people speculate that God created mankind for His entertainment. The idea was that He plopped humans down on earth and then sat back on His heavenly throne with a bowl of popcorn to see how we would do. Some believe He takes a hands-off approach, while others think He's keeping score, rewarding us now and then when we get things right and punishing us when we get things wrong.

What a difference it makes to realize that God did not create simply *because He could*, to know that the world isn't some cosmic experiment or source of entertainment for our heavenly Father.

God created out of *love* for *love*.

Let the implications of that truth sink in.

Our all-powerful Creator God is intensely and fundamentally relational. By extension, we, too, are intensely and fundamentally relational because we are made in God's image. This is why, deep in our hearts, each one of us—male and female—longs to be pursued. We want to be desired and sought out by one who loves us. We want to be seen, known, and valued for who we truly are. We want to know that we are welcomed and wanted.

In the brokenness of this fallen world, however, we too often experience wounds created by transactional

God created out of love for love.

relationships. Instead of being loved, we are abused by someone wielding oppressive power, used for someone else's gain, or neglected or abandoned by those who are supposed to love us most. Feeling damaged and defeated, we can't comprehend being worthy of anyone's attention, much less that of the Creator of the World.

But guess what? God created you out of love and for love—for relationship with *Him*. To God, your worth isn't based on your accomplishments or failures. Your value is not in your actions but in being His creation. You do not have to earn God's love; He gives it freely. His greatest desire is for you to know Him and love Him—and to let Him love you right back.

*For in Him all things were created: things in heaven and on earth, visible and invisible, whether thrones or powers or rulers or authorities; all things have been created through Him and **for** Him.*
—Colossians 1:16, NIV
(emphasis added)

But . . . ? An Anticipated Question

But wait. If God created out of love for love, does that mean God was lonely or needy? If things were so perfect between the Trinity, why create in the first place?

(Here we go again, ascribing our human nature to God's perfect character.)

No, God was not lonely. Nor did God *need* the world or people; He has no lack, only abundance.

*The LORD, the LORD, the compassionate and gracious God, slow to anger, **abounding in love** and faithfulness . . .*
—Exodus 34:6b, NIV
(emphasis added)

God is so full of all that is good that it overflows and spills out of Him. Imagine pouring water into a cup but not stopping even when it is full. The water flows over the top and onto the table. So it is with God. He overflows with all that is good, and out of that overflow, He made the world.

The earth is full of His unfailing love.
—Psalm 33:5b, NIV

As the culmination of His good work, God created mankind in His image and offered humanity an invitation into the circle of perfect love, grace, goodness, and community enjoyed by the Trinity. God wanted to share that beautiful experience of love, purity, and goodness.

To some extent, I'm sure you can relate to God's desire to share something you love. Maybe it's a television show or movie that you find so satisfying or enjoyable that you immediately tell your friends about it. You want them to experience the joy you felt when you watched it.

To an even grander degree, so it was with God! God did not create because He was lonely or needy. He created out of love, for relationship, which He had in abundance! He desired to share the beauty He was experiencing within the Trinity.

> For thou hast created all things, and **for thy pleasure** they are and were created.
> —Revelation 4:11b, KJV
> (emphasis added)

Here's the Good News: Love is the beginning.

This brings us back to the beginning: God created because He is intensely and fundamentally relational.

In my search to understand how the gospel is good news for today, I cried out to God for answers. I wanted a resolution for the trials that had caused my world to crumble. I needed a balm for the ache in my heart. I begged for a ray of light to break through the darkness.

His answer was *love*.

Understanding that God's love and desire for intimate connection was the catalyst for creation touched my heart deeply. Knowing that God created each of us so we could know and love Him, and so He could love us, changed the way I viewed myself and my relationship with Him.

As I glimpsed into the creation aspect of the gospel, I recognized my habit of approaching God *transactionally* instead of relationally. Far too often, I sought to *earn* His love and favor rather than simply *experiencing* it.

But I couldn't earn what I already possessed. Neither can you.

God cannot love you any more than He does right now. Nor can He love you any less. He created you because He desires a relationship with you. He created you out of love, for love.

God loves us *unconditionally*. That means our worth is not based on our accomplishments or our failures. Our value is being His carefully crafted and treasured creation.

He loved us *first* because God *is* love.

That's the *full* gospel truth, and it is very good news indeed.

* How to Make a Proper London Fog

1. Bring ⅔ cup water to a boil, remove from heat, and add 1 Earl Grey tea bag and ½ tsp. dried lavender (optional).
2. Cover and steep for 3–5 minutes.
3. Combine 1 ½ teaspoons sugar and ¼ teaspoon vanilla in a mug.
4. Pour the tea into the mug and stir.
5. Heat ⅔ cup milk with a frother and pour into the mug.
6. Spoon the froth on top and sprinkle with more dried lavender or cinnamon if desired.

Chapter 4

Created for His Presence

I will make my home among them. I will be their God, and they will be my people.
—Ezekiel 37:27, NLT

And I heard a loud voice from the throne saying, "Look! God's dwelling place is now among the people, and he will dwell with them. They will be his people, and God himself will be with them and be their God."
—Revelation 21:3, NIV

My dad went to divinity school (a fancy name for a school where you study religion) in the 1960s. By the time I was born, our home library contained Bibles in a variety of languages. As a little girl, I would try to impress my friends by declaring (falsely), "I can read Greek *and* Hebrew!"

To prove my fabricated linguistic skills, I would pick up one of my dad's Greek or Hebrew Bibles, turn

An Ancient Text with a Specific Purpose

Before we go any further, I need to make this clear: To truly understand the whole story of Scripture, we must recognize that the Bible is an ancient text written to a particular people who lived in a particular time and place. More to the point, while the Bible was written for us, it was not written to us—us being twenty-first-century Christians in the Western world. If we insist on reading the Bible from that point of view, we'll either miss treasures of truth or, worse, misunderstand them. If we want to grasp hold of its truth and depth of meaning, it is our responsibility to make the necessary efforts to understand the cultural and historical context of the book. We need to, as best as we can, view Scripture from an ancient Near Eastern perspective and work to read these inspired words the way the original readers would have read them.

As Sandra Richter explains in her book *Epic of Eden*, "The God of history has chosen to reveal himself through a specific human culture. He used Israel's culture as a vehicle through which to communicate the eternal truth of His character and His will for humanity." As such, "we must understand the vehicle through which it was communicated."[40]

When we are willing to look at Scripture through the eyes of its original readers, we can gain a better understanding of the complexities and beauty of God's story.

to the first page, and "read" what I had memorized: "In the beginning God created the heavens and the earth."

I don't think anyone bought it.

Church-going children everywhere have Genesis 1:1 memorized. (The words have been around so long that even many non-church-going people can quote them!) From Sunday school flannel board stories and youth group apologetic gatherings to becoming a Sunday school teacher and reading the Bible with my children, I became so familiar with Genesis 1 and 2 that when it was time to read Genesis for myself, I often skimmed (or skipped) those chapters. I thought those first couple of chapters were just backstory, not *the* story.

What I understand now, however, is that the gospel begins in Genesis 1, not Genesis 3. The story of creation matters for so many reasons, but not the one some people expect. The account of the shaping of this world, the people who live in it, and the universe that holds it is not there to explain creation in scientific terms or recount a play-by-play of the action. The book's author, directed by God's Holy Spirit, wrote Genesis 1 and 2 using words and depictions that would communicate specific things about God to the original audience.

What did God create?

When we put on an ancient Near Eastern lens, we see so much more going on in the creation story than we may have previously realized.

Just as pondering the *why* of creation deepened our understanding of God, we can learn more about our Creator by considering this question: *What did God create when He made the heavens and the earth?*

I'm not making this up.

Despite having grown up in the church and being somewhat well versed in Scripture, until just a few years ago, I hadn't heard any of what I am going to share with you in this chapter. So, it doesn't surprise me when I share this content that some people look at me skeptically and question, "Are you making this up?"

Let me assure you: I am not making this up. I understand the question, though, because, wearing my modern-day Western lenses, I might have asked the same one not long ago.

In my search to discover the meaning of the gospel for my life today, I learned from and read books by scholars who focus on understanding Scripture in its context. Scholars such as N.T. Wright, Ray VanderLaan, Kenneth Bailey, Sandra Richter, Tim Mackie, Richard Middleton, Scot McKnight, John Walton, Michael Heiser, and G.K. Beale. (See the appendix for a list of these resources.) These scholars opened my eyes to the depth and beauty we discover in God's Word when we read it the way it was intended to be read.

The answer may seem obvious. After all, Genesis chapters 1 and 2 list exactly what God created: the sky, sea, land plants, sun, moon, stars, fish, birds, animals, and finally, humans.

Yes, yes. All of that is correct. But there is another answer to the *what* question.

Let's ask the question a different way: *What is the first chapter of Genesis showing us that God created when He made the heavens and the earth?*

The answer might surprise you.

God created a home.

God built a *cosmic temple* as a place for His creation and Him to live together. Because (remember) God is intensely and fundamentally relational. He didn't just want to create humanity; He wanted to dwell with those He created in love, for love.

God's Cosmic Temple

If you're anything like me, you might have already reached for your phone to pull up Genesis 1 and 2 on your Bible app or started flipping through the first few pages of your Bible trying to figure out how in the world *cosmic temple* could be the right answer to the *what* question of creation. But I'll tell you right now, you're not going to find the words *cosmic temple* in your Bible.

The creation story does not specifically include those words, but it didn't need to for its original audience to understand that was the message. The story *showed* it.

For anyone unfamiliar with the ancient cultural context (which is most of Western society), the meaning of Genesis 1 and 2 is easy to miss. If we're more focused on trying to use the text to prove the scientific validity of creation, we miss the main point of Genesis 1, which, as Richard Middleton, a professor of biblical worldview and the Old Testament explains, is "that this world is God's intended dwelling, which He has sanctified with His presence."[1]

A Familiar Ancient Idea

While the idea of this world being a cosmic temple (or *creation* temple) may sound foreign to us, it's a familiar concept to ancient Near Eastern cultures. Language in other passages of the Bible hint at this concept as well; for example, in Proverbs, man's building of a house and God's creation of the world are described using similar terms and ideas. Consider the similarity of these two passages depicting a man building a house and God creating the world, using the architectural terms *founded* and *established*:

> *By wisdom a house is built,*
> *and by understanding it is established;*
> *by knowledge the rooms are filled*
> *with all precious and pleasant riches.*
> —Proverbs 24:3–4, ESV

> *The LORD by wisdom founded the earth;*
> *by understanding he established the heavens;*
> *by his knowledge the deeps broke open,*
> *and the clouds drop down the dew.*
> —Proverbs 3:19–20, ESV

God also used architectural imagery when He questioned Job:

> *"Where were you when I laid the foundation of the earth?*
> *Tell me, if you have understanding.*
> *Who determined its measurements—surely you know!*
> *Or who stretched the line upon it?*
> *On what were its bases sunk,*
> *or who laid its cornerstone*

when the morning stars sang together
and all the heavenly beings shouted for joy?"
—Job 38:4–7, NRSV

Other biblical authors used architectural metaphors to describe God's creation:

- The prophet Amos said God "builds His upper chambers in the heavens and has founded His vaulted dome over the earth" (Amos 9:6, NASB).

- Isaiah said that God is the one who "stretches out the heavens like a curtain, and spreads them like a tent to dwell in" (Isaiah 40:22, ESV).

Several verses refer to the foundations of the earth:

- Psalm 102:25, NIV: "In the beginning you laid the foundations of the earth, and the heavens are the work of your hands."

- Proverbs 8:29, NLT: "I was there when he set the limits of the seas, so they would not spread beyond their boundaries. And when he marked off the earth's foundations."

And finally, the psalmist brings many of these images together in Psalm 104, "portraying God's fashioning of the world as the construction project of a careful craftsman:"[2]

Praise the LORD, my soul!
LORD my God, you are very great;
you are clothed with splendor and majesty.
The LORD wraps himself in light as with a
garment;
he stretches out the heavens like a tent

*and lays the beams of his upper chambers on their
waters.
He makes the clouds his chariot
and rides on the wings of the wind.
He makes winds his messengers,
flames of fire his servants.
He set the earth on its foundations;
it can never be moved.*
—Psalm 104:1–5, NIV

As Warren Austin Gage notes in his book *The Gospel
of Genesis*, "The Hebrew Bible is replete with descrip-
tions of creation as a tabernacle which God has pitched
(Psalm 104; Job 9:8; Isaiah 40:22), or a house that God
has established (with pillars, windows, and doors: Job
26:11; Gen 7:11; Psalm 78:24)."[3]

Not Just Any Building

God's act of creation was the building of a home. God
established this world as a place for Him to dwell. We
call God's dwelling place a temple; thus, we can view
the world as a cosmic temple.

Tim Mackie, co-founder and lead research scholar
of the Bible Project, explains that the three-tiered construction of sky, land, and water that God used to build
His Temple also held special meaning for the original
audience of the creation story:

Tier 1—Sky

The first tier of God's cosmic or creation temple is the
skies, also known as the heavens. People long ago did
not have the knowledge of the universe we have today,
so their understanding of the cosmos was different.

An Ancient's Understanding of the Biblical Creation

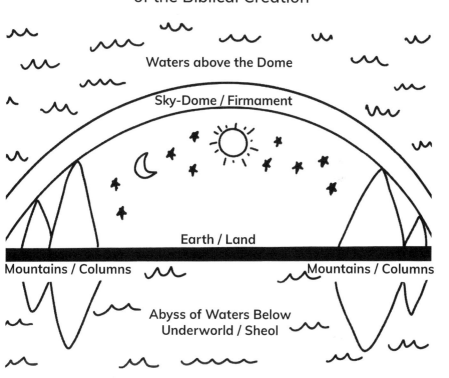

Back then, when a person looked up at the blue sky, they believed they were seeing water held behind a sky-dome (firmament) that had been placed to separate the waters above from the waters below. Recall Amos 9:6 (NASB); God "builds His upper chambers in the heavens and has founded His vaulted dome over the earth." They believed God was enthroned in His heavenly temple above, and the world beneath was the floor of His throne room.

Another way of looking at the three tiers of creation is as three circles within each other, moving from the waters to the land with the skies in the middle.

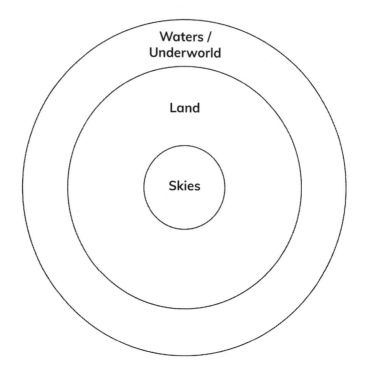

Tier 2—Land

The land is the second tier of the creation temple. When the chaotic waters were separated, dry land appeared. The water above was held behind the sky-dome, and the land floated on and was bordered by the sea. The mountains on the land supported the sky-dome.

Tier 3—Water

The third tier of the creation temple is the waters, or as it was also called, the underworld. Ancients believed that the waters beneath the land were dangerous. As such, this third tier is associated in the Bible with the grave, the pit, and *Sheol*.[4]

Understanding this imagery is important because, as we will see, God repeatedly uses this pattern. From the earth to Eden, to the Temple, God's dwellings characteristically consist of three distinct sections with increasing degrees of holiness as one draws nearer to the presence of God. The images on the following pages depict these three tiers as the first hearers of the creation story might have understood it.

The Symbolism of the Seventh Day

The creation story culminates on the seventh day, and it's a significant day for several reasons. We don't have to have a complete understanding of ancient Near Eastern culture to know that the number seven holds special meaning in Scripture.

When we read in Genesis 2:1–3 that God rested from all His work on the seventh day, we may (joking or not) think, *Well, no wonder! He must have been tired from doing all that creating!* Even if we know God does not sleep,* we tend to breeze past these verses and deem them an example set for the Jewish practice of Sabbath rest.

But take a look at what we miss by reading this passage without our ancient Near Eastern lens.

Closing Day

If you've ever bought or built a house, you know the thrill of closing day. It's the long-anticipated day you officially take ownership of your new home. After signing mountains of paperwork, you take possession of the keys and then, suddenly, the structure transforms

---

*   Psalm 121:3–4

in both purpose and value from being a house to being *your home.*

The phrase *God rested* has nothing to do with the Creator being tired or wanting to take a day off. The rest described on the seventh day depicts the completion and the taking of possession of the home God had built for Himself. "God finished the job and then took up residence to enjoy what he had built. God made a world—a heaven and earth together world—in which to dwell."[5]

John Walton, professor of Old Testament at Wheaton College, explains in his book, *The Lost World of Genesis One*, that part of the reason the inclusion of the seventh day and the mention of rest are critical components of the creation story:

> Genesis 1 can now be seen as a creation account focusing on the cosmos as a temple. It is describing the creation of the cosmic temple with all of its functions and with God dwelling in its midst. This is what makes day seven so significant because without God taking up his dwelling in its midst, the (cosmic) temple does not exist. The most central truth to the creation account is that this world is a place for God's presence.[6]

Richard Middleton describes the importance of God resting on the seventh day this way: "The very point of God's 'rest' in Genesis 1 (and in Ancient Near Eastern creation accounts) is that having constructed the cosmos as his 'house' or temple, the divine King has now taken up residence in the world. God is now sitting on his throne, reigning as Lord of the universe."[7]

By taking possession of His cosmic temple, God establishes His authority over and ownership of His dwelling place.

But hang on, there's more.

Installation Day

The seven days described in the creation story also point to the practice of temple dedication. Walton explains:

> *In the Ancient Near East, temples were typically dedicated in a seven-day ceremony with the god coming to 'rest' in his temple once it was complete and his image was installed. . . . The account [in Genesis 1 and 2] can then be seen as a seven-day inauguration of the cosmic temple, setting up its functions for the benefit of humanity, with God dwelling in relationship with his creatures.*[8]

When a temple was dedicated to a god in a non-Jewish culture in the ancient Near East, an idol would be installed to represent that god's image. But God had another plan for His cosmic temple. Using words that the original audience for this story would understand, He described His intention for creation—and humanity. Instead of placing an inanimate statue in His cosmic temple to represent His divine image (something God's people would have recognized as a pagan practice), God created humanity to bear His image.

God created humanity to bear His image.

> *Then God said, "Let us make mankind in our image, in our likeness, so that they may rule over the fish in the sea and the birds in the sky, over the livestock and all the wild animals, and over all the creatures that move along the ground."*
>
> *So God created mankind in his own image, in the image of God he created them; male and female he created them.*
>
> —Genesis 1:26–27, NIV

God created mankind in His image and placed them in His creation temple as His image bearers. Humanity is a living image of the divine Creator and King!

A Day Intended for Eternity

Notice, too, that the account of each of the other days of creation ends with the statement, *And there was evening, and there was morning the [first, second, third, etc.] day.* The omission of this phrase on the seventh day is intentional. *The seventh day was not meant to have an end.* With the completion of His perfect cosmic temple and His image bearers, God intended to live with His people and rule together forever.

Eden: A Sacred Place

In Genesis 2, the focus shifts specifically to the second tier of the cosmic temple: the land. Here, the story portrays God as a gardener who, as with the cosmic temple, creates and orders the land into three tiers of varying degrees of holiness: the center of the garden where God placed the tree of life (Tier 1), the rest of the Garden of Eden (Tier 2), and the land of Eden (Tier 3), with the unordered dry land outside. As such, we see that within the cosmic temple, God created an Eden temple.

The Eden Temple

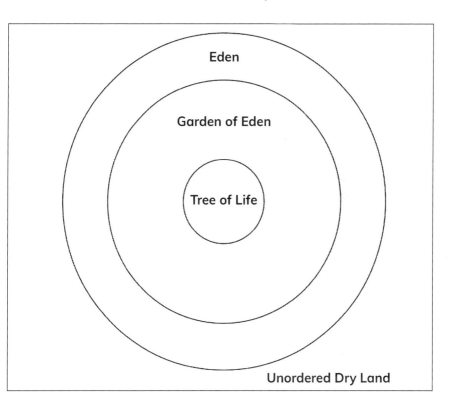

In the garden, Adam and Eve fully experienced God's presence as they walked and talked with God*— building and growing the relationship for which they were created. With full access to their loving Creator, they lived in the beauty and holiness of His creation. Eden was God's perfect plan realized. It was as Richter notes, "the *people* of God, in the *place* of God, in the *presence* of God."⁹

---

*   Genesis 3:8

God's presence saturated the garden. In this sacred space, Heaven and Earth overlapped.

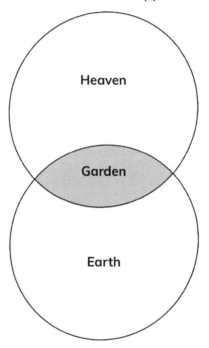

Here's the Good News: God still wants to dwell with humanity.

The story of creation outlined in Genesis 1 and 2 is about so much more than setting the scene or proving God's power. As we look at this story in the context of its original ancient Near East setting, we see a rich, deep meaning that extends beyond facts to God's purpose for the people and place He chose to create. The intentional telling of this story reveals that God built a temple, a home, where He could dwell among His creation.

So how does understanding this add to our appreciation of the full gospel? Why is it good news? Because God's intentions have not changed.

The design of creation, Eden, and Adam and Eve as image bearers of the all-mighty, all-powerful Creator gives us a clear picture of God's perfect plan for the world—and for each of us. His love-driven desire was to give humanity access to His presence and goodness in a way that can seem hard to experience or even imagine in our broken world today. But the good news of this story for us is that God still desires to walk in that closeness with us.

As we move into other aspects of the gospel—the *Fall* and God's *Redemption*—we'll see that His saving grace gives us access to His Spirit, His Holy presence in

God's intentions have not changed.

our day-to-day lives. And as we look at the *Restoration* that comes with the full gospel, we'll discover that God's original, perfect plan is still His intention for us for eternity—and today.

Before we get there, however, we need to address one more question regarding another *what* of creation: *What was God's original calling for mankind?*

Chapter 5

Created with a Calling

Then God said, "Let Us make mankind in Our image, according to Our likeness; and let them rule over the fish of the sea and over the birds of the sky and over the livestock and over all the earth, and over every crawling thing that crawls on the earth."
—Genesis 1:26, NASB

Therefore, go and make disciples of all the nations, baptizing them in the name of the Father and the Son and the Holy Spirit. Teach these new disciples to obey all the commands I have given you. And be sure of this: I am with you always, even to the end of the age.
—Matthew 28:19–20, NLT

Have you ever wondered why you're here?

Not here, reading this book, but *here* in this world. I'm going to risk assuming that this age-old question has at least crossed your mind. Maybe you don't dwell on it, but if you do, you're not alone. Countless self-help books, social media quizzes, and therapy sessions focus on this one question: *What is my purpose?*

In the previous chapter, you got a clue to that question's answer, albeit on a global scale: God created mankind to bear His image. You might be thinking, *what does that even mean?* And if you're asking *that* question, once again, you aren't alone; in fact, the previous chapter might have left you with more questions than answers! Questions like the ones I asked:

- What does it *mean* for mankind to be created in the image of God?
- What were Adam and Eve *to do* as image bearers?
- What was God's original *calling* for mankind?
- How does knowing that help me understand *my* calling?

Once again, we'll turn to the first two chapters of Genesis for answers.

Made in God's Image

So God created mankind in his own image, in the image of God he created them; male and female he created them.
—Genesis 1:27, NIV

Humans are the *imago dei* (a Latin phrase meaning "image of God"). In contrast to the rest of creation, God made mankind in His image and likeness. As such, we possess certain qualities:
- We have a soul.
- We are creative.

- We are consciously aware.
- We have the privilege and ability to have a relationship with God.

These qualities, among others, are what make us human. They also offer insight into what God is like. Understanding these traits, however, doesn't answer the question of what it *means* to be an image-bearer. For that, we need to turn to Scripture to learn how bearing the image of God fits into the story of God—particularly the story of creation and the original call on mankind. Let's start with what God says when He announces His intention to create mankind:

Let us make mankind in our image, in our likeness,
so that *they may rule over the fish in the sea and the birds in the sky, over the livestock and all the wild animals, and over all the creatures that move along the ground.*

—Genesis 1:26, NIV
(emphasis added)

Don't read that verse too quickly. Do you see the two words "so that" nestled in the middle? Those two words are critical. They signal that as image bearers, we have a specific task. It's a job that only humans, those made in God's image, can accomplish: the task of ruling.

In his book *The Liberating Image,* Richard Middleton explains that the term *image of God* describes "the royal office or calling of human beings as God's representatives and agents in the world." Being made in the image of God means humans have been given "power to share in God's rule or administration of the earth's resources and creatures."[10]

Cultural Context

Remember that Scripture was written with a particular people in a particular cultural context in mind. The original recipients of the creation story immediately understood God's message when He said, "Let us make mankind in our image, in our likeness, so that they may rule . . ." They knew that a king's image (a statue) conveyed his authority wherever it was found. When placed around the kingdom, the statues ensured citizens and foreigners alike knew who ruled the region, even when the king himself wasn't around.

God wanted Adam and Eve, as royal priests, to care for and protect the sacred space of Eden–the temple where they dwelled in relationship with Him.

Similarly, worshippers and priests placed idols in their homes and pagan temples to represent the gods they worshiped. The idols weren't considered gods; they simply bore the god's image and served as reminders of the deities.

This context gives us a better understanding of God's intention for mankind as image bearers. Having been made in His image, mankind was appointed and given authority to rule over the earth and take care of all that God made (rule = royal duties) while also showing everyone and everything who God was and what He was like, by being like Him (representing God = priestly duties). God placed humans in His cosmic temple to be His kingly and priestly representatives in the world.

Let's turn back to Scripture and see how this unfolds.

Original Calling

God created Eden and planted a garden in it. Everything inside the garden, from the trees to the rivers, reflected abundant life in God's presence. Then God placed Adam and Eve in the garden to "work it and keep it." Their job was to partner with God to uphold that beauty and order by taking care of the garden.

The Hebrew word for "to work" can be defined as you may imagine it—to cultivate the soil. The same word is also translated as "to serve" and "to worship." Likewise, the Hebrew word "to keep" is also translated as "to guard," "to keep watch," and "to protect." The words show up later in Scripture to describe the priestly task of guarding the Tabernacle and protecting it from anything that might corrupt the sacred space; in fact, the only other place where these words—*to work* and *to keep*—are used together in Scripture is to describe the priestly duties of the Levites serving in the tabernacle.

God wanted Adam and Eve, as royal priests, to care for and protect the sacred space of Eden—the temple where they dwelled in relationship with Him.

But that was only part of their calling.

Expanding the Beauty and Order of Eden

Scripture identifies Eden as a specific piece of land on Earth, land which God formed, filled, and ordered. The same peace, beauty, and order that existed inside the garden did not, however, exist outside of it.

What was to be done about that? In Genesis 1:28, we are given a glimpse of God's intentions through His instructions to Adam and Eve when He says: **"Be fruitful and multiply, and fill the earth, and subdue it; and rule over [it] . . ."** (NASB, emphasis added).

It's easy to skim over familiar verses like this, but let's break it down and look closely at its meaning.

"Be fruitful and multiply, and fill the earth, and subdue it; . . ."

This first part of God's directive is clear: Adam and Eve were to have children who would have children who would have children, and so on. As the family grew, they were not to remain in the piece of land described in Genesis 2:10–14. Instead, Adam and Eve's descendants gradually were to fill and populate the earth. God wanted His creation to partner with Him in bringing peace to disorder.

As usual, however, there is depth beyond the surface-level meaning of this passage. The Hebrew word for *subdue* means "to conquer" or "to bring into subjection." What did Adam and Eve and their descendants need to conquer and subdue? As mentioned above, they were to bring peace to the chaos found outside the garden. But that's not all. Satan, whose presence brought darkness and disorder, was also on the earth at that time. As such, they were also to conquer the enemy, disguised as the serpent, whose desire was to pervert God's good world and return it to darkness and disorder.

". . . and rule over [it]."

As the *imago dei*, mankind had a unique role as God's representatives in creation. They were to rule or have dominion over the earth. God empowered Adam and Eve with His authority to rule, reign, and represent Him to the world.

How would Adam and Eve be equipped to subdue and rule? Through relationship with their Creator, by loving God and learning life at His feet. They would love others as He loves, love themselves as God loves them, and love the world He gave them by being good stewards of all contained within. They would subdue, or bring order to, the land by using their God-given gifts to create, design, build, and expand God's Kingdom by keeping Him at the center of everything. This means they would rule, bring order to the disorder outside of Eden, and protect the ever-expanding nature from anything that threatened its sacred space in keeping with God's character of love.

Sandra Richter says it this way:

> *This was Adam and Eve's perfect world. Not just fruit and fig leaves, but an entire race of people stretching their cognitive and creative powers to the limit to build a society of balance and justice and joy. Here the sons of Adam and the daughters of Eve would learn life at the feet of the Father, build their city in the shadow of the Almighty, create and design and expand within the protective confines*

*of His kingdom. The blessing of this gift? A civiliza-
tion without greed, malice, or envy; progress without pollution, expansion without extinction. Can you
imagine it? A world in which Adam and Eve's ever-expanding family would be provided the guidance they
needed to explore and develop their world such that
the success of the strong did not involve the depri-
vation of the weak. Here government would be wise
and just and kind, resources plentiful, war unnecessary, achievement unlimited and beauty and balance
everywhere. This was God's perfect plan: the people
of God in the place of God dwelling in the presence
of God.*[11]

God loved the beauty, goodness, and joy He experienced within the Trinity so much that He wanted to
share it. With that desire in mind, He built a house.
Then, out of the overflow of His goodness, He made
mankind in His image because He wanted relationship
with them. Then God placed them in His home.

His love was (and is) so great, He wanted to expand
the boundaries of this place where Heaven and Earth
coexisted—the garden. He knew that the bigger this
place was, the more people could dwell in His presence
for relationship. So, God gave Adam and Eve the job
of keeping the garden, ruling over the earth, and sub-
duing it. Using the building blocks of relationship and
love, they were to expand the reach of His Kingdom.

With Adam and Eve as His image bearers, God
didn't need to place inanimate statues throughout His
expanding kingdom; in fact, later, God specifically pro-
hibited the use of idols of any kind. His calling was for
humanity to spread His love, goodness, and peace by

representing Him and reminding everyone in whose kingdom they dwelled.

Here's the Good News: God's plan has not changed.

The original calling for mankind was to partner with God to not only sustain the order God had established in the Eden temple but also to spread it. Adam and Eve and all of their descendants were to expand the borders of the Eden temple, the place where Heaven and Earth intersected, until it covered the whole earth.

Adam and Eve were to bring the Kingdom of Heaven "on earth as it is in heaven" (Matthew 6:10). That was God's original plan. That was our fundamental calling as human beings and our purpose as image bearers and royal priests—to preserve, protect, and expand the sacred space.

Again, the good news is that God's plan has not changed. It is still our call today to bring peace to chaos and order to disorder. It is still God's desire for His kingdom to cover the whole world. We aren't here, as I previously believed, to sit around and wait for Jesus to return to set things right. We are meant to partner with Him and work to set things right. Like Adam and Eve, our calling is to use our God-given gifts to create, design, build, and expand God's Kingdom by keeping Him at the center of everything.

If this role in God's Kingdom sounds too big, especially in light of the darkness of the world around us, take heart. God doesn't expect you or me to fulfill that mission alone. In fact, He promises to be with us every step of the way.

The Fall

Chapter 6

From Blessed to Cursed

So the LORD God banished them from the Garden of Eden, and he sent Adam out to cultivate the ground from which he had been made.
—Genesis 3:23, NLT

The kingdom of heaven is like a king who prepared a wedding banquet for his son. He sent his servants to those who had been invited to the banquet to tell them to come, but they refused to come.
—Matthew 22:2–3, NIV

Imagine that you're hosting a dinner to celebrate moving into your dream house. You designed the home to be a place where everyone you love dearly can gather and enjoy one another. Everything is ready: You've carefully designed each detail with your guests in mind. You've brought out the best dishes and set the most beautiful table. You've made sure to include everyone's favorite foods on the menu—in abundance. Enticing aromas and comfortable chairs beckon your guests to come, relax, and enjoy.

Each person you have invited possesses wonderful talents. Today, as a part of the festivities, the artists, engineers, scientists, teachers, doctors, and writers will enjoy the gifts of the musicians you've asked to share a song after dinner. You can imagine how the music will fill your new home, blessing everyone inside. You've put your heart into the preparations because you want the dinner to be a wonderful experience for all.

Can you imagine the joyful anticipation?

The perfect evening has been carefully planned and each of your guests has been offered their invitation. They are eager with anticipation and excitement and, yet, still free to make other plans. You know the tension well, don't you? Doing everything you can and knowing that it is still up to someone else to decide to show up?

Invited by God

"The people of God, in the place of God, in the presence of God." That was God's perfect plan, and everything was in its place for God and mankind to reign and rule together forever:

God's people, fearfully and wonderfully made in His image, would partner with Him as royal priests.

God's dwelling place brought Heaven and Earth together and provided abundance for life and purpose for His image-bearers as they worked with Him to preserve, protect, and expand the sacred space.

God's presence offered love and community—perfect relationship—for and with His creation.

God created the perfect kingdom, the perfect conditions for a beautiful life and eternal relationship. In His mercy, He gave Adam and Eve explicit instructions and boundaries from the very start. They could eat from every tree in the garden but one. The consequences were clear: If they ate the fruit forbidden by God, they would die.

And the LORD God commanded the man, "You are free to eat from any tree in the garden; but you must not eat from the tree of the knowledge of good and evil, for when you eat from it you will certainly die.
—Genesis 2:16–17, NIV

God created Adam and Eve to trust Him. If they did, He offered life, in His presence, in this beautiful place He had designed. He wanted relationship with them.

God also wanted that relationship to be their choice, so He gave Adam and Eve the freedom to trust themselves. If they did, they would forfeit the life He offered. They would die.

Did they want to live with God forever, fulfilling their calling and purpose as image bearers and royal priests—or not? Did they want the world He had created for them—or not?

Life or death?

Blessing or curse?

The choice was before them.

Before the Fall

Bringing order to disorder, peace to chaos and spreading the rule of Heaven throughout the earth sounds daunting. But God had given Adam and Eve authority and power (because authority is necessary to rule) as His image bearers so they could accomplish their calling. Their authority was linked to their faith in the Creator—the one who would teach and instruct them daily to live justly and act mercifully. The more they chose to depend on God and partner with Him, the more His blessing and goodness would flourish in and around them. It sounds idyllic and, perhaps, impossible given the current state of our world. Remember, though, that the earth was different before the Fall. Unhindered by the curse and consequences of sin, the land was ready to yield to the work of their hands.

Before the Fall, the world wasn't under Satan's power.* Sure, he existed, but he was a created being just like Adam and Eve. Unlike God's image bearers, however, Satan had no power or dominion on Earth. Nor did he have any authority over mankind. Adam and Eve didn't need instructions on spiritual warfare or lessons on how to defeat the devil and his demons; in fact, they didn't even need to give Satan a thought.

And Satan knew it.

A Cunning and Deceitful Enemy

Satan, a created spiritual being, wanted to *be* God rather than live under God's wisdom and authority. Knowing that he lacked the power to defeat God, he went after what God loved and had made in His image: mankind. He wanted the dominion that God had given Adam and Eve, so he was going to have to get it from them. But he couldn't charge into the garden and take it by force; his only weapons were his words.

---

*   1 John 5:19

Just like he does today, Satan used words to plant doubts of God's goodness in Adam and Eve's minds.

Just like he does today, Satan used words to plant doubts of God's goodness in Adam and Eve's minds. He craftily twisted the meaning of God's words and implied that their Creator was holding out on them—that there was something better available God didn't want them to enjoy.

Satan's purpose was to convince Adam and Eve to agree with him in direct opposition to God. If he could get their agreement, he could acquire the power he coveted.

(By the way, Satan uses the same tactics today. We give him power by agreeing with his deceitful and damaging words, by listening to the lies he whispers and allowing them to repeat in our minds instead of actively silencing them. But without our agreement, he is powerless.)

The Fall

We know what happened next: Adam and Eve listened, agreed with, and obeyed the serpent. And when they did, they forfeited their God-given authority and instead found themselves under the authority of the one who had distracted and deceived them, the serpent.* Adam

---

*   Romans 6:16

and Eve's position of rule and dominion became part of the devil's spoil, enabling him to kill, steal, and destroy.* At that moment, a clash of two kingdoms began: the kingdom of man vs. the Kingdom of God. This was the beginning of a cosmic battle that still exists today.

Suddenly, mankind became powerless to fulfill God's assignment to subdue and rule the earth. Having relinquished the authority God had given them, the task was now humanly impossible.

It was a mistake—a *choice*—with devastating consequences.**

Instead of ruling over the serpent, Adam and Eve subjected themselves to the serpent, giving him the power to rule over them.

Instead of carrying and cultivating God's peace, beauty, and order, Adam and Eve became a part of Satan's plan to spread mistrust, violence, sin, and death to the world.

Devastating Consequences

Adam and Eve's disobedience and submission to Satan came at a devastating cost. Because of their choice, Adam and Eve could not remain in the garden with access to the tree of life, so they were exiled and cast into the dry land where disorder and Satan reigned.***

> *And the LORD God said, "The man has now become like one of us, knowing good and evil. He must not be allowed to reach out his hand and take also from the tree of life and eat, and live forever."*
> —Genesis 3:22, NIV

---

*   Romans 6:16
**   Genesis 3:14–19
***   1 John 5:19

Instead of living in a world full of goodness, joy, beauty, and life, their world was cursed with loss, anxiety, violence, and death.

Instead of guarding and growing Eden as royal priests, cherubim with a flaming sword guarded Eden against them.

This movement from blessing to curse is called the *Fall* (or we could just as easily call it the *choice*). The Fall is the second part of the full gospel—the part that introduces the problem of sin and separation from God. The repercussions affected the entire cosmos, including all of humanity, from that moment forward. With the Fall, humans lost their identity as God's people, their place in His perfect and abundant Eden temple, and their access to His presence. Intimacy and relationship—the very things for which God created humanity—were broken, *shattered*.

> *With the Fall, intimacy and relationship—the very things for which God created humanity—were broken,* shattered.

Why does God offer a choice?

Before we move on to the good news (and there is really good news), let's pause here. This story, too, is a part of Scripture that was so ingrained in me that my familiarity with the story blocked me from asking questions about it as I matured. I just accepted it at face value. Rabbi David Fohrman, in his book *The Beast That Crouches at the Door*, calls this unthinking acceptance the *Lullaby Effect*. He proposes that because we are so familiar with childhood lullabies, we don't stop and think about their words. Take, for instance, "Rock a Bye Baby." In a sweet, gentle voice, we sing, "when the bough breaks, the cradle will fall, and down will come baby, cradle and all." How is that imagery conducive to a good night's sleep? It isn't! But most of us don't think about the violence of those words. We stopped listening to them long ago because we've heard and sung them since childhood.

Rabbi Fohrman says that we often treat Bible stories the same way. That in almost every major story there is an *"elephant in the room*—some major problem, or a series of them, that cries out to be addressed. . . . But the stories are too familiar to us. We've heard about them so many times, they've become part of our cultural fabric. We absorb the stories through osmosis, the way we unthinkingly develop accents that reflect the place where we grew up. We fail to see the problems anymore."[12]

In his book, Fohrman encourages his readers to not fear asking questions, because they are not really problems, but *opportunities*:

> *They are windows that the text gives us to perceive its deeper meaning. Sure, you can keep the*

window closed and pretend it isn't there. But if you don't open it, the treasure that lies beyond—a richer, three-dimensional understanding of the [Scripture] . . . will remain sealed off to you forever. . . . Read the stories slowly and carefully. And as you do, ask yourself these questions: If I were reading this for the first time, what about it would strike me as strange? What are the 'big questions' that the [Scriptures] want me to ask about this story? What are the elephants in the room?[13]

The first three chapters of Genesis, when we stop to think about them, can stir up some pretty big questions, *especially* for those who don't understand God's heart:

- *Why would God create a paradise and then tempt Adam and Eve with the forbidden tree?*

- *Why would God want to deny them knowing good from evil?*

- *Would we be better humans without that knowledge?*

- *What would a world be like with people who didn't know right from wrong?*

- *Was it really fair to banish them from Paradise after one mistake?*

- *Was this just a setup? And why didn't they die right away, as God seemed to imply?*

Those are the kinds of things I wondered before I understood the first part of the story. Without knowing the *why* behind creation or understanding that creation is an essential part of the gospel, I had my doubts about God's motive for giving Adam and Eve such an impossible choice.

If we think of the creation story as simply an explanation for the first human beings, we run into a problem. But if we consider that the Holy Spirit prompted the author of Genesis to write this story in a way that would clearly communicate to the original audience (the young nation of Israel) what it meant to live in the Kingdom of God, we can see more of what is going on. In Chapter 8, we'll also see how Adam and Eve's story offers a preview of the story of Israel and its choice to follow God's Law (the Law of Moses) and dwell in the Promised Land—or not.

Trust or disobey? Life or death? Blessing or curse?

God offered Adam and Eve a choice in the sacred space of the Garden of Eden.

He offered a choice to the Israelites at the foot of Mount Sinai.

And God offers a choice to you and me today.

But let's not get ahead of things. Let's get back to those two trees in the garden and why God offers this choice in the first place.

The tree of life and the tree of the knowledge of good and evil provided what could only be given by God: life and wisdom. Many scholars propose that God didn't place the restriction to not eat from the tree of the knowledge of good and evil because knowledge of good and evil is wrong or because He didn't *ever* want them to know the difference between good and evil. He did, in fact, want them to know, *eventually*, and He wanted them to gain that knowledge *His* way. God's way requires trust, reverence, and love, words that can be summarized in the phrase "fear the Lord." It is when we fear the Lord that we gain true knowledge and the wisdom to use that knowledge as God intends.

*The fear of the LORD is the beginning of
knowledge.*
—Proverbs 1:7, NIV

Following God's path to wisdom brings *life.*

*Blessed are those who find wisdom, . . . She is a tree
of life to those who take hold of her.*
—Proverbs 3:13a, 18a, NIV

John Walton says,

> *We make a mistake to think that this is simply
> about magical trees in a garden paradise. It is about
> the presence of God on earth and what relationship
> with him makes available. . . . God is the source and
> center of wisdom—not us. . . . Life and wisdom are
> possessed by God, and they are made available to
> humans as they are in relationship to him. The trouble
> comes when humans try to seize wisdom on their
> own terms.*[14]

Life and wisdom that come through relationship
with God serve and spread the Kingdom of God.

Life and wisdom that come by man's own terms
serve and spread the kingdom of man.

When Adam and Eve disobeyed God and took the
shortcut offered by the serpent, they chose whom to
serve.

Adam and Eve's choice to eat from the tree doomed
them to die. Physical death did not come right away,
but they did immediately lose access to the tree of life
when God exiled them from the garden. We often think
of the banishment as a consequence of their sin, and
it was. But it was also an act of God's mercy. If they

had continued to eat from the tree, they would have remained in a state of sin, and God loved them too much to allow that to happen.

Here's the Good News: God has a rescue plan.

How could there be good news in this part of the gospel? The plan failed. Humanity and all of creation fell under the curse of sin and death. What's good about that? Is the good news that God had a Plan B?

No. Eden was the perfect plan, and it has never stopped being so. As Richter wrote in *The Epic of Eden,* "God's original intent is His final intent. His goal was that the people of God might dwell in the place of God, enjoying the presence of God. This is all our heavenly Father has ever wanted for us. And everything that lies between Eden's gate and the New Jerusalem, the bulk of our Bibles, is in essence *a huge rescue plan.*"[15]

What God intended at creation, God will see done. That, my friend, is the good news.

God's desire for a relationship with those made in His image has not wavered.

Even though mankind rebelled against Him, God remains faithful. His love and His calling for mankind are unchanged.

Even though mankind lost access to the tree of life, there will be a day in the new heaven and new earth when we will enjoy the fruit of the tree of life for all eternity.

Knowing, however, that sin made mankind's calling humanly impossible, God set His rescue plan in motion.

Redemption

Chapter 7

God's Rescue Plan

Noah and Abraham

When God made his promise to Abraham, since there was no one greater for him to swear by, he swore by himself, saying, "I will surely bless you and give you many descendants." Because God wanted to make the unchanging nature of his purpose very clear to the heirs of what was promised, he confirmed it with an oath. God did this so that, by two unchangeable things in which it is impossible for God to lie, we who have fled to take hold of the hope set before us may be greatly encouraged.

We have this hope as an anchor for the soul, firm and secure.

—Hebrews 6:13–14, 17–19a, NIV

It is for freedom that Christ has set us free. Stand firm, then, and do not let yourselves be burdened again by a yoke of slavery.
—Galatians 5:1 NIV

I was born into a church-going family. Any time the church doors were open, I was there. I could name the sixty-six books of the Bible before I could read, and by elementary school, I was quite competitive in Bible Drill (a race to find a specific Bible verse the fastest). I knew all the famous Bible stories, and by the time I was in high school, I was teaching them to other children.

Life shook my seemingly rock-steady, Bible-centric world right about the time I went to college, and I was not prepared for the changes. While I was away, my parents divorced after twenty-eight years of marriage. My brother, an addict, went to jail. At the same time, I was dealing with the pain of being rejected by the university I had dreamed of attending.

Life was not turning out as I had expected.

What still surprises me is that, in the midst of this difficult season, I never once considered praying for help or looking in my Bible for answers. Somehow, despite growing up surrounded by people who loved God and poured so much into me, I didn't believe the Bible was relevant to daily living.

Goodness gracious. Am I the only one, or have you been there as well?

To me, Bible stories were just that—*stories*. Well, stories and *rules*. I failed to see how a story about a man building a big boat and ushering in two of each animal was going to help me with any part of my life. And what good did it do to follow the rules? I had been a "good girl" my whole life, but that didn't earn me protection from rejection and pain.

And prayer? I didn't know God in that way. I prayed for the missionaries overseas, for God to bless the food, and to save others from their sins. Wasn't that what the church was all about, making sure everyone gets to heaven?

Hmm . . . do you see a theme? My interaction—my only real relationship—with God was transactional. For me, a transactional relationship was as good as religion got.

I had no idea back then that God is intensely and fundamentally relational. Nor did I understand the story of the Bible, God's story. To me, the Bible was sixty-six books that were only connected by the cover and a few main characters. What I didn't know then is that those sixty-six books come together to reveal a God who relentlessly pursues His creation. A loving Creator who, from the very beginning, had a rescue plan. Who, despite rejection time after time, continued to pursue, forgive, and restore, only to have to go through that same cycle over and over again.

Since then, I have learned three important things that changed everything about living as a Christian today:

1. The Bible *is* relevant.
2. The Bible is *not* a rulebook.
3. The Bible is the story of *love*. A love that is determined to exist free from any and every hindrance, compromise, or manipulation. A love that gathers the rebels, orphans, and misfits along the way, offering wisdom and freedom for all who trust in the One who *is* love.

If I had only known. And understood. And trusted.

And, oh, if only Adam and Eve had known God for who He is and had understood and trusted His goodness. If only they had confidence concerning His plans for them!

Would they have made a different choice? Who knows? What we do know is that God refused to *force* mankind to love Him; that wouldn't really be love.

If God had been driven by power to create, rather

God refused to force mankind to love Him; that wouldn't really be love.

---

than love, He might have said, "Oh, well. Mankind is so frail. Now that sin has been given power in the world, creation will only disappoint me over and over and over again. I'll just scrap it all and keep enjoying what exists among the Trinity."

Thank goodness our all-powerful God *is* love. Love didn't (and doesn't) give up on humanity. In essence, His response to Adam and Eve's choice of sin was as if He said, *I know you made a mistake, and that mistake has changed the world and everything between us. But you are worth fighting for. I love you and want to be in relationship with you. I want to be loved and known by you. Nothing will stand in My way. Although the consequences of your decision will be felt throughout the ages, I will stop at nothing to rescue you. I will redeem you and restore my original plan to live with you. Your mistakes do not change My love for you.*

Hope for *All* Mankind

God had a rescue plan. Right in the middle of Adam and Eve's rebellion, God offered hope—hope for them, their descendants, indeed, hope for all of creation and mankind.

That hope was the Promised One: the Curse Breaker and Liberator of the world.

Before God cast Adam and Eve out of the garden, He made it clear how the victory over sin would come. He promised that Eve's offspring would one day crush Satan and ensure the safety and freedom of the world. This Promised One, the Messiah or Savior, would do what Adam did not. In crushing the head of the serpent, this *new* Adam would restore the blessings of Eden.* God would fulfill His original plan to dwell with His creation in loving relationship. "The people of God, in the place of God, dwelling in the presence of God."

God's people clung to the hope that the Promised Messiah would set all things right. Passing that hope from generation to generation, many, but sadly not all, actively waited and watched for His arrival. The stories in the Old Testament foreshadowed the Savior's arrival as God worked through specific people to advance His rescue plan. Woven into those stories, we see the thread of redemption.

At times, it seems the plan took two steps forward and one step back, but little by little, His plan advanced toward fulfillment. In the following two chapters, we

---

*   Genesis 3:15

will look at how God's rescue plan unfolded in the lives of Noah, Abraham, Moses, and David.

Noah: Reestablishing Relationship
Genesis 6–9

Noah's story begins ten generations after Adam, and by the time he comes on the scene, the world is unrecognizable in comparison to Eden. Which is why God doesn't have many nice things to say about the state of the world during Noah's time. Look at how Scripture describes it:

> *The Lord saw how great the wickedness of the human race had become on the earth, and that every inclination of the thoughts of the human heart was only evil all the time. . . . Now the earth was corrupt in God's sight and was full of violence. God saw how corrupt the earth had become, for all the people on earth had corrupted their ways.*
> —Genesis 6:5, 11–12, NIV

Pay close attention here: Just like in Genesis 1, the Lord *saw*, but this time He didn't see anything good. Instead, *every* inclination of the thoughts of the human heart was *only* evil *all the time*. The world seems dark now, but when I consider this scripture, I realize that the state of today cannot compare to the depravity of Noah's time. How far humanity had fallen from the purity and beauty experienced in the Eden temple!

This was not what God wanted for His creation. Can you imagine the heartache God felt as He faced rejection after rejection from the crown of His creation? God was filled with regret as His image bearers spread evil, corruption, and violence instead of His loving kingdom. Grieved, God sent a flood, an *un*-creation event, to "wipe from the face of the earth the human race I have created. . . ."

". . . *But* [such an important little word] Noah found favor in the eyes of the Lord" (Genesis 6:7–8, NIV). Protecting Noah and his family and two of each animal—just enough for a new beginning on earth—God started over with His creation.

After the flood, with Noah and his family back on dry ground, God blessed them and gave them a calling and a promise. The calling was the same one He had given Adam and Eve: "be fruitful and increase in number; multiply on the earth and increase upon it" (Genesis 9:7, NIV). As a new Adam, Noah's role was to spread God's Kingdom and fill the earth with His goodness.

Then God made a promise, one that we still benefit from today. Even though God knew mankind would continue to reject Him, God would not curse the earth again because of man or destroy all living creatures.* The rainbow would be a visible sign in the sky to remind us of this promise.

By intervening in Noah's life, blessing him with a calling and a promise, God reestablished His relationship with mankind. It was the first step of His rescue plan.

---

*   Genesis 8:21–22

A Clash of Kingdoms

If only Noah and his descendants had known and understood and trusted God and His goodness. Instead, they trusted in themselves. Rather than filling the earth as God directed or glorifying Him as His image bearers, they acted in direct defiance of God's command and schemed to remain in one location and glorify themselves saying, "Come, let us build ourselves a city, with a tower that reaches to the heavens, so that we may make a name for ourselves; otherwise we will be scattered over the face of the whole earth" (Genesis 11:4, NIV).

The choice to reject their role as image bearers for God's Kingdom came at a cost. God diffused their power by confusing their language and scattered mankind over the face of the whole earth.

With the damage done, the clash between the Kingdom of God and the kingdom of man continued.

Abraham: A Promise for All People
Genesis 12–24

Years passed and the kingdom of mankind grew, as did the grip of violence and wickedness. God's heart toward mankind, however, remained constant. Our faithful and unchanging God held to His promise and His plan to rescue creation. Moving that plan forward, God chose the family through whom the Promised Messiah would come.

In Genesis 12, we meet Abram and his wife, Sarai. Abram (whose name God later changed to Abraham)

Intense and Persistent Faith

Chutzpah is a Hebrew word that has taken on a negative tone today. If someone has chutzpah, they may be viewed as pushy, intense, or aggressive. One of the root words of chutzpah, however, is faith. Not faith as in "I understand and believe this," but faith as in, "I am going to hold on to this promise and will not let it go." It's an intense and persistent kind of faith. It's not unlike the more modern phrase like a dog with a bone.

A person with chutzpah will not quit, give up, or let go. The depth of his faith combined with his familiarity with God gave Abram the confidence—the chutzpah—to ask, "Where's the son you promised?"

lived in Ur, a city that was located in what is now southern Iraq. God appeared to Abram and called him to leave his country and family—everything he had ever known. Without giving Abram a specific destination, God set him on a journey with a promise:

I will make you into a great nation, and I will bless you; I will make your name great, and you will be a blessing.
I will bless those who bless you and whoever curses you I will curse;
and all the people on earth will be blessed through you.
—Genesis 12:2–3, NIV

Despite not knowing God until that day, Abram trusted Him and obeyed. He packed up his household and traveled to the land that God showed Him.

God's call on Abram's life, combined with Abram's obedience, changed the course of humanity.

Down the road (literally), God revealed another facet of His rescue plan. When Abram and his caravan reached Canaan, God appeared to him and said, "To your offspring I will give this land" (Genesis 12:7, NIV). Abram's descendants would come to know this as the Promised Land.

God appeared to Abram several times in the years that followed, often either reaffirming or expanding His promises. One significant encounter is found in Genesis 15, just after Abram had returned victorious from a battle that, if not for God, he should have lost. He had taken 318 trained men with him to rescue his nephew Lot from four kings and their armies and had returned victorious. Recognizing God's provision, Abram gave a tenth of the spoils to Melchizedek, king of Salem, a "priest of God Most High" and rejected a generous offer from the king of Sodom whose people he had rescued along with Lot.*

Imagine what Abram might have been mentally and emotionally processing when he returned to his tent that night.

- He might have worried about retaliation from the defeated kings.

- Perhaps he reflected on the truth that God had won the battle for him.

---

*   Genesis 14

- He could have been wondering how he would explain to the trained men who had risked their lives in battle for him why he had rejected the spoils and rewards of battle that the King of Sodom had offered him.

Between the worry and the letdown after the adrenaline rush of battle, it would have been difficult to rest.

Knowing Abram and his need, God appeared to him in a vision and said, "Do not be afraid, Abram. I am your shield, [I am] your very great reward" (Genesis 15:1, NIV). With those words, God affirmed that He was Abram's protector, so there was nothing to fear. Nor did he need the spoils or rewards of war because God Himself was his great reward.

God had promised Abram land, children, and the Messiah (although that part of the promise was in code: "Through you all the nations of the world will be blessed."). Believing those promises, Abram and his wife, Sarai, waited for children. And waited. And waited.

When God reaffirmed His promise and status as Abram's very great reward, his response sounded something like this: "Thanks, God, but where are the kids? You promised me children! Since I don't have any, everything You have given me will go to my servant when I die!"

Abram knew. He understood. He trusted God. In fact, Abram didn't just know *about* God, He *knew* God. He had an intimate and deeply personal relationship with Him.* Because their relationship was personal and he trusted fully in the goodness and faithfulness of God's character, Abram spoke to God with *chutzpah*.

---

*   2 Chronicles 20:7

God was not offended by Abram's question. Instead, He was honored by Abram's faith. In return, God honored Abram by giving him the assurance he needed.

In response, God told Abram to go outside and look up at the star-filled night sky. Remember, there was no light pollution. Can you even imagine? Nothing to distract from the darkness of the night sky or the brightness of a universe full of stars. "Count them," God said, "if indeed you can count them." Then God told Abram that one day, his descendants would be as numerous as those stars.

Scripture tells us Abram believed God, and God credited that faith to him as righteousness.*

But God didn't stop at affirming His promise for children. God went on to remind Abram that He would give him the land as far as he could see.

For a tent-dwelling nomad, God's promise probably seemed unimaginable. He had seen Canaan's richness—and had just battled with the armies of four of the many kings who lived there.

Since God hadn't seemed to mind Abram's *chutzpah* before, he asked God, "How can I know that I will gain possession of it?"**

God's answer was, in essence: *Do You want to know how you can know? I'll show you exactly how you can know for sure. If that is your need, I will meet it.*

What He actually said was, "Bring me a heifer, a goat and a ram, each three years old, along with a dove and a young pigeon" (Genesis 15:9, NIV).

To us, that might not seem like an answer to the question Abram had asked, but Abram immediately

---

*   Genesis 15:4–6, NIV
**   Genesis 15:8, NIV

understood the request. He gathered the animals and prepared them for a familiar covenant ritual. He cut the animals in half and arranged the halves opposite each other so that as the blood drained, it formed a pool—a blood path—between the pieces.

This custom sounds strange to us, but to the people of that time, *karat berit,* or cutting covenant, was a solemn, unbreakable vow. Unlike promises today that are easily broken, often without consequence, a covenant had a weightiness that we don't understand.

But Abram did.

Cutting covenant was a relationship—not simply an agreement—between a greater (*suzerain*) party and a lesser (*vassal*) party. The greater party set the terms of the covenant, and the lesser party could accept or reject them. If accepted, both walked through the blood path, with the *suzerain* leading the way, as a way of saying, "May what was done to these animals be done to me if I do not keep this covenant."

Cutting covenant was, and actually still is, a very common practice in the desert communities of the Middle East. I once heard Bible scholar Ray Vander Laan explain during a teaching session how this "blood path rite" was used to arrange a marriage. He had seen the ceremony performed while living with a Bedouin family.

Just as Abram had many millennia earlier, the lesser party—in this case, the bride's father—gathered the animals, cut them in half, and laid them out. Then the greater party—the groom's father—took off his shoes, picked up his robe, and stomped through the blood. Without saying a word, the groom's father conveyed a powerful message: If my son is not everything

I promised—a provider, a good leader, etc.—then you may do this or worse to me.

Next, the bride's father took off his shoes, picked up his robe, and walked through the blood. The silent action spoke for him: If my daughter is not all I promised—pure, faithful, etc.—then you may do this or worse to me.

With this covenant made, the punishment for any fault of the son or daughter fell on their fathers.

Vander Laan explained that even today, this covenant holds incredible meaning—and consequences. It is not unusual to find the father of the one who failed in the marriage with his throat slit in the desert with footsteps in his blood.

Knowing all of this, perhaps it's not surprising that Abram felt a "thick and dreadful darkness" (a Hebrew colloquialism that means scared out of your mind) come over him as he fell into a deep sleep. After all, he was the (far) lesser party in a blood covenant with the Almighty God of the universe.

With the sun beginning to set, Abram fell asleep watching the blood drain from those animals to create a path and wondering about (or perhaps dreading) the terms of the covenant.

Many scholars believe God had already told Abram what He expected of him. They think the terms are being restated in Genesis 17 when God reaffirmed His promise by changing Abram's name to Abraham and adding circumcision as a sign of the covenant between God, Abraham, and Abraham's descendants. God began then by telling Abraham to "walk before me, and be blameless, that I may make my covenant between me and you, and may multiply you greatly" (Genesis 17:1b–2,

ESV). If Abram believed that his and his descendants' blamelessness before God was part of the terms for the covenant, it's no wonder a wave of dread washed over him. The track record for mankind was not good! How could Abram not just promise but *covenant* that he and his descendants would walk blamelessly before a perfect and holy God?

But God, in his wildly lavish love, stepped in and took all the responsibility and the burden for fulfilling the covenant Himself.

But God, in his wildly lavish love, stepped in and took all the responsibility and the burden for fulfilling the covenant Himself.

God, the greater party, said without words, *Abram, I love you so much that I am going to give you a son, land, descendants, and the Promised One to save the world. If I don't keep my word, then you can do this to me.* The message to Abram and any ancient Near Easterner would have been unequivocal. God, as a smoking firepot, symbolically trampled barefoot through the blood to give Abram the assurance he needed to trust God's Word *without a doubt.*

Then it was time for Abram, the lesser party, to walk through the blood path. If I were Abram and knew that the terms of the covenant were for me to be blameless before God, I would be shaking in fear. I would know that the moment I stepped into the blood, I was sentencing myself to death *and* forfeiting the promises of land, descendants, and the Messiah. Abram knew there was no way he could keep his end of the covenant.

That's when God did something that Abram wasn't expecting. God took Abram's place.

Symbolized by the blazing torch, God passed again through the blood. Without words and with no room for doubt, God took full responsibility for the covenant. The message was clear: *Abram, you are not held responsible for this covenant. This is mine to bring about. If you sin, if you are not perfect, if your descendants are not blameless, if you break the covenant in any way, you may do this to* **me**.

In that moment, God sentenced Himself to die.

Just as God promised Noah that he would not destroy the earth with a flood again, knowing full well that mankind would continue to sin, God stood in for Abram. He knew Abram and his descendants would not be blameless but would, instead, sin and reject Him again and again. God also knew the price He would pay one day on the cross.

A Promise for All People

A year before the birth of their promised son, God changed Abram and Sarai's names:

Abram, which meant "exalted father," became Abraham, "father of a multitude of nations."

Sarai, which meant "my princess," became Sarah, "mother of nations."

With these new names and the blessing of their son, Isaac, God also gave Abraham and Sarah new identities as the new Adam and Eve. Their role gave them and their descendants purpose: They were to bear God's image and multiply His kingdom, starting in their Eden, the Promised Land. They were to show others who God is and what He is like by being like Him.

God's promise and His covenant and complete responsibility to fulfill it meant that one day, Abraham's family tree would include the Promised Messiah. And through this descendant of Abraham, God continues to bless all people.

Here's the Good News: God's love and His promises are unchanging.

God's rescue plan is full of good news for you today. The biblical accounts of Noah and Abraham offer promises and hope that you can hold on to.

Your mistakes do not change God's love for you. Just as God did not abandon Adam and Eve when they sinned, He will not abandon you. He promises that if you search for Him with all of your heart, you will find Him.* There is nothing you can do to make Him love you more than He does right now, and there is nothing you can do to make him love you any less. God's love is unconditional.

God works through imperfect people. In the stories of the Old Testament, we see that the people God worked through are truly human beings—they make

---

*   Jeremiah 29:13

mistakes—sometimes *big* mistakes. But when they confess and return to God, He is gracious to forgive and restore. "If we confess our sins to him, he is faithful and just to forgive us our sins and to cleanse us from all wickedness" (1 John 1:9, ESV).

God is a covenant making, covenant keeping God. His words stand forever. What He has promised, He will bring to fruition. He will do everything He said He will. You may not know when or how, but you can be certain He will.

Chapter 8

Renewing Hope

Moses and David

He reached down from on high and took hold of me: he drew me out of deep waters. He rescued me from my powerful enemy, from my foes, who were too strong for me. They confronted me in the day of my disaster, but the LORD was my support. He brought me out into a spacious place; he rescued me because he delighted in me.

—Psalm 18:16–19, NIV

From Noah to Abraham, God's rescue plan advanced and expanded.

- In Eden, every man, woman, and child had full access to God's presence. After the Fall, all were excluded.

- After the flood, God recommissioned humanity through one man, Noah.

- Through Abraham and his descendants, God identified His *people* through one family and established their *place*—the Promised Land.

But God wasn't done. His plan, though progressing, had not been fulfilled—yet. As we review this familiar story, notice how Moses fulfills his role in this stage of God's dual-purpose rescue plan.

Moses: Rescued for Relationship

Exodus and Deuteronomy

When Moses came on the scene, the descendants of Abraham had been enslaved in Egypt for centuries. This is quite a drastic change from where we ended the previous chapter, but it wasn't a surprise to God. Generations earlier, God warned Abraham what was to come.

> *Know for certain that for four hundred years your descendants will be strangers in a country not their own and that they will be enslaved and mistreated there. But I will punish the nation they serve as slaves, and afterward they will come out with great possessions.*
> —Genesis 15:13–14, NIV

Escaping a famine, the descendants of Abraham had moved to Egypt hundreds of years before. While living there, they multiplied so greatly that their large number alarmed Egypt's ruler, Pharaoh. Fearing rebellion, Pharaoh enslaved them.*

---

*   Exodus 1:8–14

But just as He had promised Abraham, God heard the cry of His people. In answer, God called Moses,* an eighty-year-old prince turned shepherd, to be His representative (to bear His image) to the people and to Pharaoh. In this role and with God's authority, Moses would free the people from their oppression.

Delivering His people from Egypt was only part of God's purpose for Moses, however. In addition to freeing His people from slavery, God wanted Moses to lead them to the Promised Land, a good and spacious land, flowing with milk and honey, where they could live and prosper.** This rescue and relocation project would fulfill a promise He had made to Abraham. This Promised Land would be a new Eden where God would reign as their king.

God sent Moses to declare His promise and plan to His people:

I am the LORD, and I will bring you out from under the yoke of the Egyptians. I will free you from being slaves to them, and I will redeem you with an outstretched arm and with mighty acts of judgment. I will take you as my own people, and I will be your God.
—Exodus 6:6b–7a, NIV

When I think about the generations of people who had lived under the tyranny and abuse of the powerful nation of Egypt, I can't help but wonder what it must have felt like to hear those words. I know how easily I can become cynical. In the past, I've been quick to question God's goodness when life didn't go the way

---

*   Exodus 3:7–12
**   Exodus 3:8

I'd hoped. The Hebrews had been slaves for *hundreds of years*. What, then, was the state of their hearts? Were there some who remembered and clung to God's promises to Abraham? Had knowledge of the God of their fathers faded over the centuries for some? Did some harbor anger and unbelief in their hearts? What did it mean for them to be remembered by the Lord?

Jon Tyson, in his book *Beautiful Resistance*, notes that the words the Lord spoke to them through Moses hold an even deeper meaning when viewed through our ancient Near Eastern lens:

> When God used Moses to call the children of Israel into their destiny, he made four promises: I will take you out, I will rescue you, I will redeem you, I will take you to me. These four promises were the same four invitations a young man made to a woman on her wedding day. God was not just delivering Israel; he was proposing to her. He called her his "treasured possession" (Exodus 19:5), the same words a groom would use for his bride.[16]

Despite what some may have feared, God had not forgotten His people, nor had He forgotten the covenant He had made with their fathers. He had seen their suffering and heard their cries, and it was time for Him to move. More than simply rescuing the Hebrews, God promised the people a relationship. Remember, God is intensely and fundamentally relational.

Rescuing the people from Egypt involved many signs and wonders. The plagues displayed God's power and ultimate authority to the Egyptians and surrounding nations. At the same time, these mighty acts served to remind or reveal to God's people who He was.

After ten terrible plagues, Pharaoh finally relented and agreed to let the Hebrews go, but you know the story: As the people fled Egypt, Pharaoh changed his mind.

With Pharaoh's army chasing them down and the Red Sea blocking their escape, death or slavery seemed imminent. *But* God performed yet another wonder on His people's behalf, one reminiscent of the creation story. He separated the waters to expose the dry land, parting the Red Sea and making a path of escape. For anyone who had not known God previously, they were getting a good idea of who He was now.

Mount Sinai

Safe on the other side of the Red Sea, God's people traveled through the wilderness until they stopped at Mount Sinai. There, Moses repeated the Lord's proposal to His bride Israel, and God initiated the marriage covenant.

> *You yourselves have seen what I did to Egypt, and how I carried you on eagles' wings and brought you to myself. Now if you obey me fully and keep my covenant, then out of all nations you will be my treasured possession. Although the whole earth is mine, you will be for me a kingdom of priests and a holy nation.*
> —Exodus 19:4–6, NIV

God had freed His people and brought them out of Egypt in order to bring them to Himself. He then invited them to become what He had created mankind to be: a kingdom of priests within the Kingdom of God. Priests who would bear God's image to the world around them while expanding God's Kingdom. This time, it wasn't a person or a family that God chose to take up Adam and Eve's calling; it was a nation, the newly formed nation of Israel descended from Abraham.

As He had done with Adam and Eve, God gave His people a choice. For Adam and Eve, the choice was to trust God and obey His directive to not eat from the tree of the knowledge of good and evil. Obedience was the condition for remaining with Him in Eden.

At Mount Sinai, God promised the Israelites that if they would choose to keep His law in this new kingdom, they would be His treasured possession, a kingdom of priests, and a holy nation. Again, obedience was required to be a part of the Kingdom of God.

The Israelites accepted the terms of the covenant; in fact, their initial, enthusiastic response was, "We will do everything the LORD has said" (Genesis 19:8b, NIV).

A Different Kind of Kingdom

God's Kingdom was different from that of the pagan nations that surrounded them; indeed, it was different from anything they had ever seen or experienced. Born and raised as slaves, the Israelites had no other context for life than the evil and violent oppression they had experienced in Egypt. They didn't know how to live or interact with others in healthy or godly ways, much less rule as a kingdom of priests.

God's people needed to unlearn the ways of Egypt and learn the ways of God. If lived out correctly, their lives, in contrast to the kingdoms around them, would attract others, thereby expanding God's Kingdom. To equip this chosen nation to fulfill its role as the new Adam who would bear His image, God gave Moses specific instructions for His kingdom. These instructions,

which became known as God's Law or the Law of
Moses, introduced the people to the God of their fathers,
Abraham, Isaac, and Jacob, and taught them what God's
Kingdom should look like. More than that, the Law outlined the terms of the marriage covenant between God
(the *suzerain*, or greater party) and the nation of Israel
(the *vassal*, the lesser party).

Moses relayed God's terms to the people, and again,
they agreed to do everything the Lord commanded.
Then, at the foot of Mount Sinai, God entered into a
marriage covenant with the nation of Israel. Moses
set up an altar where the people brought their animal
offerings to the Lord. He sprinkled half the blood from
those offerings on the altar and then read God's covenant terms once more to the people. Once more, the
people said they would obey all that God had spoken.
With that agreement, Moses sprinkled the people with
the other half of the blood from the offerings and said,
"Behold the blood of the covenant that the LORD has
made with you in accordance with all these words"
(Exodus 24:8, ESV).

A New Dwelling Place

With the covenant between God and His people confirmed, God invited Moses, the priests, and the elders to
meet Him on Mount Sinai to share a meal. Participating
in a common practice for a covenant ceremony, these
leaders enjoyed the very uncommon experience of eat-
ing and drinking in the presence of God.*

Then God called Moses higher up the mountain
while the priests and elders stayed where they were.
The glory of the Lord settled on Mount Sinai and

---

*   Exodus 24:9–18

covered it with a cloud. Moses remained at that mid-point on the mountain for six days. On the seventh day, God called to Moses from within the cloud, and Moses climbed higher, into the cloud—and even closer to God. On the seventh day, *just like the seventh day of creation,* God and man met where, because of God's presence, Heaven and Earth became one.

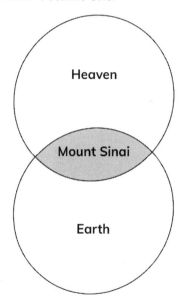

In that heaven-and-earth space on the top of Mount Sinai, God gave Moses specific instructions on how to build the Tabernacle, a traveling temple where God could dwell with His people as they journeyed to the Promised Land.

Listen to the heart of the Father longing to live with His creation once again:

> *Have them construct a sanctuary for Me,* ***so that*** *I*
> *may dwell among them.*
> —Exodus 25:8, NASB
> (emphasis added)

God desired *to live among His people.*

Patterned after God's heavenly temple, the Tabernacle's design pointed back to the Cosmic and Eden temples, from its three-tiered structure to the cherubim at its entrance, to the furniture that represented different aspects of the garden. The three sections of the Tabernacle represented varying degrees of holiness: the Holy of Holies, the Holy Place, and the Outer Courtyard, and also paralleled the ascension on Mount Sinai.

Holy of Holies

Just as Moses was the only person God permitted to come into His presence at the top of Mount Sinai, only the high priest would be permitted to enter the Holy of Holies in the Tabernacle.

The Holy Place

God invited the priests and the elders up the slope of the mountain to partake in a covenant meal. They were near enough to God's presence to see Him, but there was still a degree of separation. The Holy Place offered a similar nearness to the Levitical priests whom God chose to serve in the Tabernacle.

The Outer Courtyard

During the marriage covenant and covenant meal, the people of Israel remained at the foot of Mount Sinai where Moses built an altar and set up twelve pillars representing the twelve tribes of Israel.* The Outer Courtyard of the Tabernacle provided a similar space for gathering, for offering sacrifices on the bronze altar, and for cleansing and atonement.

---

*   Exodus 24:4

A CONSISTENT PATTERN

	Cosmic Temple	Eden Temple
TIER 1	**Skies**	**Tree of Life in the center of the Garden** • All people have access to God
TIER 2	**Land** • Trees • Animals • Humans	**The Garden of Eden** • Open to all people
TIER 3	**Sea**	**Eden and the land outside the garden**

Note the parallels between the Cosmic Temple, the Eden Temple, Mount Sinai, the Tabernacle, and the Temple.

Mount Sinai

Tabernacle / Temple

Summit of Mount Sinai
- Only Moses has direct access to God

Holy of Holies
- Only High Priests can enter

Slope of Mount Sinai
- Accessible to elders and priests

Holy Place
Accessible to elders and priests
- Menorah = Tree of Life
- Cherubim = Animals
- Priests = Humans

Foot of Mount Sinai
- Accessible to everyone (Israelites)

Outer Courtyard
Accessible to everyone (Israelites)
- Bronze Laver / Sea

Mount Sinai

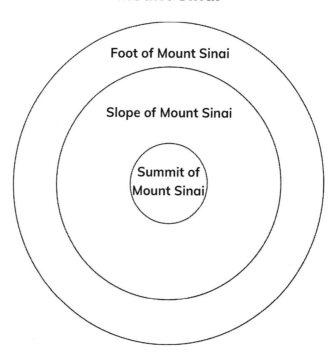

Foot of Mount Sinai

Slope of Mount Sinai

Summit of
Mount Sinai

The Tabernacle was a step forward in God's rescue mission that would redeem and restore His original plan. Upon the Tabernacle's completion, "the cloud covered the tent of meeting, and the glory of the LORD filled the tabernacle" (Exodus 40:34, ESV). Once again, Heaven and Earth overlapped. When God's people entered the Tabernacle, they inhabited two places at once. For the first time since Eden, God dwelled with His people. Sin, a problem not yet fully dealt with, still separated mankind from God, but God had made a way for people to be in His presence.

The Tabernacle

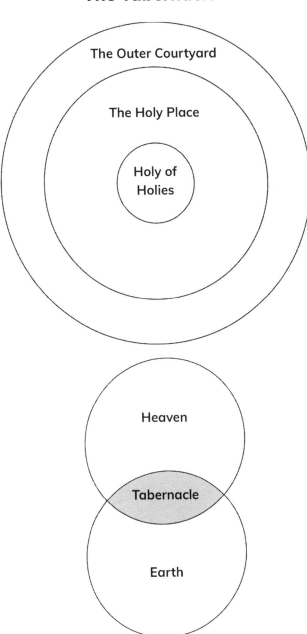

A Step Forward and a Step Back

At Mount Sinai, the nation of Israel became a new Adam. The descendants of Abraham were to be a renewed humanity, living in an alternate kingdom from the kingdom of man, picking up the original call given in the garden to bear God's image and fill the earth with children who had children who had children—all of whom would spread God's light to those living in spiritual darkness. In this way, they were to expand the Kingdom of God until it covered the earth.

Yes, it was a step forward in the plan. And then . . .

Less than two months into the union, God's people failed to honor the marriage covenant. While Moses was with God on Mount Sinai receiving instructions for building the Tabernacle, the people became anxious and fearful. From their vantage point at the foot of the mountain, the glory of the Lord looked like a fire devouring the top of Mount Sinai. Fear and anxiety replaced their faith, and they lost trust in the One who had led them out of Egypt and through the Red Sea. Moses had been gone for forty days, and they feared he was dead.

Despite God's proven faithfulness, they believed He had abandoned them in the wilderness. So they did the very thing God had commanded them not to do. They made an idol to worship, something they could see and touch—something of their own design.*

Now, before we cast judgment on this newly formed nation who found themselves in a barren wilderness without a leader, can we agree that in a world of instant gratification, forty days is a long time? Actually, forty days is a long time *any* time. And as for their short

---

*   Exodus 32:1–7

memories? I confess that I am also guilty of being surprised when God moves, *even though He has worked through my life faithfully for forty-nine years!* Sometimes throwing Israel under the bus makes me feel better about myself, when in fact, I am just as guilty as they.

At this point, God could have destroyed the people for their disobedience and what amounted to adultery. A god whose only motive was power might have. Indeed, His wrath burned against them. While he was still on the mountain, Moses showed the same kind of *chutzpah* Abraham possessed and interceded on their behalf.* Once again, God's love for mankind prevailed. Though He would have been justified in doing so, in His mercy, God did not abandon His people. In His grace, God renewed the broken covenant.**

Because of His mercy and grace and love, God's rescue plan moved forward. With Moses as their earthly leader and intercessor, the people of God (Abraham's descendants) were on their way to the place of God (Promised Land), while experiencing the presence of God (the Tabernacle).

David: A Royal Promise
1 and 2 Samuel; 1 Kings 1–2;
1 Chronicles 10–29

In the generations between Moses and David, God's people had begun to take possession of the Promised Land. Unfortunately, they had also repeatedly abandoned their calling as image bearers and, instead, "did what was evil in the sight of the Lord" (Judges 2:11,

---

*   Exodus 32:11–14
**   Exodus 34

ESV). More than once (More than a few times!), they adopted the sinful practices of their pagan neighbors and worshiped their gods.

In response to their sin, God sent a series of judges to remind the people who He was and who they were supposed to be. Convicted, either by the judges' words or by the recurring consequences that followed their disobedience, they would come back to God. Their loyalty was short-lived, however, and it was only a matter of time before the kingdoms of man enticed them once more.

Eventually, the lure of those kingdoms caused them to reject God as their king. They wanted a human king, like the other nations. The people wanted someone they could see who would rule from a throne and fight their battles for them.* God counseled them against it, even still, they insisted.

Despite their rejection of His wisdom, God answered their request and honored their freedom to choose. After the first king and a flood of corruption, we pick up the story with David, the son of Jesse, Israel's second *human* king. Chosen by God and anointed by the Levite priest Samuel, Scripture describes David as a man after God's own heart. Despite His flaws, David loved the Lord wholeheartedly and was loyal to Him. With King David, the national boundaries promised to Abraham became a reality and brought the people of God to the place of God.

When David finally entered a season of rest from his battles, he looked around him, noting the beauty of his kingdom. Grieved that he lived in a palace while God lived in a tent (Tabernacle), he told God he wanted to build a house for Him. God answered no, but

---

*   1 Samuel 8:19–21

proceeded to promise David that He would, instead, build a house for *him*. In essence, God said, "You want to construct a building for me, but I am going to build a dynasty (house) for you." More than that, God promised David that his house, his kingdom, and his throne would endure *forever*. *

God promised David that his house, his kingdom, and his throne would endure forever.

This Son of David would be the Promised One God had spoken of in the garden—the one who would crush the serpent's head. He was the one through whom, as God promised Abraham, all nations would be blessed.

Before the Promised One's arrival, David's son Solomon picked up his father's dream to build God a dwelling place.** Solomon's Temple followed the three-part pattern of the Tabernacle, Sinai, Eden, and the cosmic temple. (See the figures on the following page.)

Likewise, the dedication of Solomon's Temple was a seven-day affair, culminating on the seventh day when God's presence filled the Temple.*** With His presence, this Temple, like those before it, became a place where Heaven and Earth overlapped.

---

*   2 Samuel 7:11–13, 16
**   2 Chronicles 2:6
***   2 Chronicles 7:1–2

The Temple

The Outer Courtyard

The Holy Place

Holy of
Holies

Heaven

Temple

Earth

Exile—Hope in the Darkness

The communion between God and His people was beautiful while it lasted; however, as Jon Tyson writes, "The challenge of loving a bride like the church [or here we can say like the Israelites] is her promiscuous heart. At times, she is seduced by the power and grandeur of the world. She often gives her heart to unthinkable ideologies and idolatry, committing adultery with the enemies of Christ. But for whatever reason, God seeks her out, restores her, and brings her back."[17]

The leaders of Israel, just as their ancestors before them, eventually rejected the Kingdom of God, preferring once again a kingdom of their own making. Instead of influencing the surrounding nations, they allowed those nations to influence them. God's chosen people, His bride, scorned Him and worshiped idols. Despite God's repeated urges through the prophets (people used by God to communicate His message) to return to Him, the people persisted in their wicked ways and even neglected the Temple.

Choices always carry consequences.

Because of the people's sin, God removed His glory and holy presence from the Temple.[*]

Then, just as He had exiled Adam and Eve from the Garden of Eden, God exiled the Israelites from the Promised Land. God allowed the nation of Babylon to conquer Jerusalem. The pagan king's army destroyed the Temple and took the Israelites captive, relocating all but a few to Babylon. Thus, God's people no longer dwelled in the place or presence of God.

---

[*]   Ezekiel 10–12

N.T. Wright explains:

> *In the story the Bible is telling, humans were created for a purpose, and Israel was called for a purpose, and the purpose was not simply 'to keep the rules to be with God' or 'to go to heaven.' Humans were made to be image-bearers to reflect the praises of creation back to the Creator and to reflect the Creator's wise and loving stewardship into the world. . . . The early humans rejected the Creator's call and command; Israel rejected the much amplified call and commands of the covenant God.*[18]

But always before us is the truth that God is a God of love, compassion, and abounding in loving-kindness. True to His nature, even while His people were in exile, God called prophets to provide hope and insight into His continued purpose. Despite His chosen people's sins, God still intended for His mission to be fulfilled. He still longed for a relationship with mankind.

Here's the Good News: God will never forget you.

God is *El Roi*, the God Who Sees.* When we feel invisible or forgotten by everyone else, we can trust that God sees us. David's words, inspired by the Holy Spirit, remind us that there is nowhere we can go to escape His presence:

> *Where can I go from your Spirit?*
> *Where can I flee from your presence?*
> *I go up to the heavens, you are there;*
> *if I make my bed in the depths, you are there.*

---

*   Genesis 16:13

If I rise on the wings of the dawn, if I settle on the
far side of the sea,
even there your hand will guide me,
your right hand will hold me fast.
—Psalm 139:7–10, NIV

Even when the descendants of Abraham were far from home, mistreated and abused, God had His eye on them. When the time was right, He rescued them once again.

No matter where we may find ourselves, be it the highest of highs or the lowest of lows, God promises that He cannot and will not ever forget us.

Can a mother forget the baby at her breast
and have no compassion on the child she has borne?
Though she may forget,
I will not forget you!
See, I have engraved you on the palms of my hands;
your walls are ever before me.
—Isaiah 49:15–16, NIV

Chapter 9

Waiting with Hope

The Intertestamental Period

The LORD will fulfill his purpose for me;
your steadfast love, O LORD, endures forever.
Do not forsake the work of your hands.
—Psalm 138:8, ESV

From Creation forward, yes, even today, God has desired to live in relationship with those He created—with you and with me. That's truly the good news, the best news. The Creator longs for a relationship with you, and because of His great love, mercy, and grace, God has been working to bring humanity back into perfect relationship with Him.

It's a good thing for us that God is faithful, unyielding in His plan, and relentless in His love. From the Fall all the way to today, mankind has made a habit of foolishly rejecting God through acts of disobedience and betrayal. Indeed, if it were up to humanity to save itself, we would have no hope. *But* God never loses sight of His plan. His intention and love are pure and steadfast.

Let's quickly review what we've covered thus far. Make a note of the ways God reintroduces hope when all seems lost:

- Adam and Eve abandoned their God-given purpose as image-bearers when they chose to surrender to the serpent. In doing so, they welcomed sin into their lives and into the world. The consequences—sin, death, brokenness, sorrow, and separation from God—and the aftershock of the curse are still seen in our world today. But God promised in the garden that one day, the serpent would be crushed; God's love would prevail.

- When sinful darkness covered the earth, God sought to reestablish His relationship with humanity through Noah. Given a fresh start and tasked with multiplying God's Kingdom, Noah's descendants, too, rejected their role. The consequence of choosing to glorify themselves rather than God caused even greater disunity and strife among the kingdoms of man and between man and God.

Generation after generation, God called His people back to Himself, back into relationship with Him.

- With Abraham, God took a different tactic. Knowing that He could not rely on mankind to be faithful, God made an irrevocable covenant with Abraham. His grace-filled promise to bless all people through Abraham's offspring is a covenant that continues to bless humanity today because it relies solely on God's faithfulness.

- God kept His promise to Abraham when He called Moses to rescue the Hebrews (Abraham's descendants) from their suffering as slaves in Egypt. In delivering the people to the Promised Land, God fulfilled yet another promise He'd made to Abraham.

- God remained faithful to His word, even when the people He had rescued rejected Him time after time, choosing to disobey Him and worship pagan gods. Almost as soon as they had entered into a marriage covenant with God, they forsook their vow. Even so, God made a way for His people to experience His presence by establishing a dwelling place among them.

- Knowing His ultimate plan to rescue and redeem humanity would fail if it relied on the fickle faithfulness of mankind, God once again made a one-sided promise, this time to David. The promise that the Messiah would be the Son of David and the everlasting King was one only God could fulfill.

Generation after generation, God called His people back to Himself, back into relationship with Him. And generation after generation, the people turned their backs on Him.

With warning after warning—through prophets, whom they often ignored—God reminded His people of

His holiness and their calling and purpose as His image bearers. Despite those warnings and the consequences of their sin, God's people repeatedly betrayed Him, their true King, by choosing to worship other gods.

None of it surprised God. He knew His people; He knew their hearts. And He warned them. Just before the Israelites entered the Promised Land, Moses reminded the Israelites of the terms of their marriage covenant with God and of the consequences if they chose not to abide by them. He ended with this:

> *See, I set before you today life and prosperity, death and destruction. For I command you today to love the LORD your God, to walk in obedience to him, and to keep his commands, decrees and laws; then you will live and increase, and the LORD your God will bless you in the land you are entering to possess. **But if your heart turns away and you are not obedient, and if you are drawn away to bow down to other gods and worship them, I declare to you this day that you will certainly be destroyed. You will not live long in the land you are crossing the Jordan to enter and possess.***
> —Deuteronomy 30:15–18, NIV
> (emphasis added)

Life and prosperity or *death and destruction*. Love and obedience have always been a choice, and God knew His people would make the wrong one. Consider the prophecy that Moses spoke over the people before they entered the Promised Land. Listen to the promise God makes to them:

> *When all these blessings and curses I have set before you come on you and you take them to heart*

*wherever the LORD your God disperses you among the nations, and when you and your children return to the LORD your God and obey him with all your heart and with all your soul according to everything I command you today, then the LORD your God will restore your fortunes and have compassion on you and gather you again from all the nations where he scattered you. **Even if you have been banished to the most distant land under the heavens, from there the LORD your God will gather you and bring you back.***

—Deuteronomy 30:1–4, NIV
(emphasis added)

After generations of slavery in Egypt and then forty long years in the wilderness, it was finally time to take possession of the land God had promised to Abraham's descendants.

. . . a good land—a land with brooks, streams, and deep springs gushing out into the valleys and hills; a land with wheat and barley, vines and fig trees, pomegranates, olive oil and honey; a land where bread will not be scarce and you will lack nothing; a land where the rocks are iron and you can dig copper out of the hills.

—Deuteronomy 8:7–9, NIV

With Moses's prophecy ringing in their ears, the Israelites crossed the Jordan River and entered their Eden. God kept His promise and delivered His people to Canaan, and in the Tabernacle and later the Temple, He dwelled among them—the people of God, in the place of God, in the presence of God.

So why did the nation end up in exile?

Because God always keeps His promises.

The people's hearts turned away from God, and they did exactly what God told them not to do. True to His word, God did what He said He would.

After 800-plus years of warnings, redirection, and many chances, God exiled the people from the Promised Land and withdrew His presence from the Temple. This time, it wasn't an angel with a flaming sword that blocked the people's return but an enemy king. King Nebuchadnezzar conquered and destroyed Jerusalem and took God's people into captivity.

The good news is that not only is God a God who will do what He says He will do, but He is also a God who goes to extreme measures to redeem His people, even when it means having to walk with them through the consequences of their choices. He doesn't avoid the long hard road (like we try to do); instead, God is in it with us no matter what we choose or what others may have chosen for us. (For, sadly, there are times in life where we have to endure the fallout of other's choices.) But no matter what, God is always with us. He is with us, picking up the pieces of our lives, grieving at the fires that burn, and *leading us into new things.*

The Return to Jerusalem—The Second Exodus

For seventy years, the Israelites lived in exile in Babylon. When Cyrus the Great, King of Persia, conquered Babylon, he declared that the Jewish people could return to their homeland, ending their exile. Only a remnant, however, chose to go back to the Promised Land. Some were too old or too young to make the journey, and some were too comfortable.

For those who returned to Jerusalem, everything was different—darker. With the city in shambles, they worked to rebuild its wall, their lives there, and, most importantly, the Temple. Without Solomon's wealth and resources, however, the new temple paled in comparison to what it had once been. Even as the builders laid its foundation, those who remembered the first temple wept, perhaps because they were keenly aware of all they had lost.*

Additionally, the remnant who returned to Jerusalem did so as citizens of another nation. Persia continued to rule over them for a time, then Greece and Rome. Living under political, military, and financial subjection, the people put their hope in the Promised Messiah, the seed of Abraham, the descendant of David. The One who, they believed, would free their nation and bring back the golden days of King David.

Life after Exile

Israel's freedom to choose resulted in their captivity. Their disobedience to God subjected them to another kingdom. In that time, God worked to teach them so that they would turn their hearts toward Him alone. Did the exile work? Did God's people finally come to understand the covenant they had with Him?

The answer: yes and no. When the Jews returned to Israel, they no longer worshiped the gods of the surrounding nations; in fact, they made changes to their worship and study of Scripture to ensure that would not happen again. As such, the Judaism (the religion of the Jewish people) after the exile was different from the Judaism they had practiced before the exile.

---

*   Ezra 3:12.

One of the biggest changes was their focus on the Scriptures. In the era of the kings, Israel neglected the Temple and had all but forgotten God's Law. When King Josiah ordered repairs to be made to the Temple, workers found the scrolls containing the Book of the Law. Upon hearing the Law read, King Josiah tore his robes and humbled himself before the Lord. *He had never heard or read the Law before that, despite God's instruction for each king to write out a copy of the Law upon taking the throne.*[*]

Neglecting the Law was a recurring habit for the Jews prior to the exile. Like King Josiah, many simply did not know the Scriptures. This reality was among the charges God brought against His people before the exile: "My people are destroyed from lack of knowledge."[**] (Does that step on your toes like it does mine?)

The Jews in Babylon and those who returned to Jerusalem understood that their disobedience had led to exile. They hadn't done all the Lord had told them to do to live as a kingdom set apart; in fact, they often did the exact opposite of what He instructed. Some of that was due to the frailty of the human heart and humanity's inclination to rebel. Some of that disobedience, however, stemmed from not knowing the Law given to them by God. After all, how can you follow what you don't know?

When the people returned from exile, they resolved to never again allow generations to fall into sin because of ignorance. To ensure everyone knew the Scriptures, the Jews created an entire system dedicated to knowing the Torah. The Synagogue and Synagogue School were part of that system.

---

*   2 Kings 22 and Deuteronomy 17:8
**   Hosea 4:6, NIV

The Tanakh

The appropriate term to use for the Hebrew Scriptures is the word *Tanakh*. This name for the Hebrew Bible is made up of the first letter of each of the three sections of their Bible:

T for Torah—the books of Genesis, Exodus, Leviticus, Numbers, and Deuteronomy. (Also referred to as the Pentateuch, Book of the Law, or the Five Books of Moses)

N for Nevi'im (Prophets)— The Books of Joshua, Judges, 1 Samuel, 2 Samuel, 1 Kings, 2 Kings, Isaiah, Jeremiah, Ezekiel, Hosea, Joel, Amos, Obadiah, Jonah, Micah, Nahum, Habakkuk, Zephaniah, Haggai, Zechariah, and Malachi

K for Ketuvim (Writings)—The Books of Psalms, Proverbs, Job, Song of Songs, Ruth, Lamentations, Ecclesiastes, Esther, Daniel, Ezra and Nehemiah, 1 Chronicles, and 2 Chronicles

The Synagogue

Although it is disputed among some, most scholars believe that the idea of synagogue started in exile in Babylon. When King Nebuchadnezzar conquered Jerusalem, Solomon's Temple was destroyed and everything in it was carted off to Babylon. As a result, the Jews lost the centerpiece of their worship. There had been no other buildings or locations where worship took place—only the Temple—and it was gone. Living in exile in a foreign land and without the Temple, they had to come up with a new plan.

The people gathered in groups to talk about God and to find a way to understand and express their faith. Eventually, they constructed synagogues, buildings where people from the surrounding community could gather. Synagogues were not meant to replace the Temple; they provided a place where people could hear and learn the Scriptures. Because the synagogue was meant for the community, different people from the community were assigned to read the text aloud at each meeting.

Each week, the people gathered at their local synagogues to hear the Scriptures read. Most people sat on the floor circling a raised platform called a *bema* where the reader stood. Benches lining the walls of the synagogue were reserved for the older and wiser members of the community. One had to be invited to sit on those benches, or *chief seats*, as they were places of honor for those who had lived a long life of obedience and, thus, served as strong role models for others.

The Torah Closet in the synagogue was a chamber that housed the Torah scrolls, also known as the Book of the Law. The weekly reading consisted of a passage from the Torah, a portion from the prophets, and a portion from the writings. When someone read from the Torah, they sat in what was called the Moses Seat.

Synagogue School

The synagogue wasn't only about a worship service once a week. It was about an entire way of life centered around the Torah. Resolved to know the Law so they would never again be disobedient, they created an elaborate system to educate future generations.

The first level of Jewish schooling was for boys and girls ages five to ten and was called *Bet Sefer*, or House of the Book. The children had classes five days a week where they would study and memorize the Torah. The instructor would often quote from the Torah, beginning with "It is written" and stop mid-sentence and point to a student. The student would then need to be able to pick up quoting right where the teacher left off without hesitation and keep going. This was the expected level of familiarity with the text by the time a child completed *Bet Sefer* (at age *ten*). After this, most Jewish children left school to learn the family trade.

The students (at this time, mostly, if not all boys) who were the best of the best were allowed to continue school in *Bet Talmud*, or House of Learning. Here, students were expected to have all the *Tanakh* (our Old Testament) memorized by age fourteen. Read that again: *all* our Old Testament memorized by *age fourteen*. (When I was a camp counselor, I had a hard time getting the kids in my group to memorize a verse a day for six days! And I won't mention my own skills or lack thereof.)

Added to the memorization drills were question-and-answer sessions between teacher and student. Students learned to be curious about the Scriptures and to answer questions with another question, demonstrating their knowledge and respect for the text. (Do you remember Jesus in the Temple when He was twelve?)

Very few students made it to the next level of schooling called *Bet Midrash*, or House of Study. If a student was gifted enough and knew the Scriptures well enough, he could apply to be a *talmid*, or disciple, of a *rabbi* (a Jewish teacher or scholar). The rabbi would question and test the student to see if he had what it took to be like him in all areas of his life because the goal of every *talmid* was to know what their rabbi knew, in order to do what their rabbi did, so they could be just like their rabbi in his walk with God. If the rabbi thought the student would not be successful, he would tell him to go back to the family business. But if he thought he could do it, the rabbi would agree to become his teacher. The *talmid* would then agree to take on his rabbi's beliefs and interpretations of the Scriptures. The rabbi's beliefs and interpretations were called his yoke, and the rabbi would tell his *talmid*, "Come, follow me." It was very difficult to reach this level of schooling. This privilege was only offered to a very few people.

This was the Judaism that arose during the intertestamental period. But what was going on in the world around them at this time?

A History Lesson

After the exile, the new Judaism was finding its identity while the world around it continued to change. Around 334 BC, Alexander the Great began his world conquest. The ruler did not just want to conquer the world; he wanted to change it. The Greeks had developed a worldview called Hellenism based on a belief that humans, not gods, were the ultimate source of truth and authority in the universe. Alexander the Great conquered the Middle East not only to build his empire but to convert the known world to this worldview he believed to be superior to all others. Greek culture targeted mankind's desire for security, luxury, leisure, and comfort.

The Greeks did not get rid of the gods. Instead, they made them in their own image. Think about Zeus, Apollo, Athena; they look like us. Although believed to be powerful, their gods were not much different from the people who worshiped them. They were not a foundation for what was true or right but were instead glorified humans to manipulate for man's own end because the world had become about man's own desires.

Hellenism did, indeed, change the world as it spread and was adopted. It was the same worldview of the Romans when they conquered Greece and took over control of Judea. (In fact, it remains the worldview of the West today.) All during that time, the Jews had to decide what to do with the unbiblical view of Hellenism. Hellenism stood in stark contrast to the Tanakh. Under the control of another world power and its worldview, how would they respond? By looking at their five responses, we better understand the world, religious ideology, and beliefs into which the Last Adam, Jesus, was born. This is the world that was waiting for the Messiah.

Five Ways the Jews Responded to Rome and Hellenism

Herodians
Approach: Go along to get along.

Herodians took the "go along to get along" approach to the rule of Rome and Hellenism. They were content to follow God but did not want their comfort, power, privilege, or influence challenged. They figured that if they were friendly with the Romans, then things would be better for them. They also believed they could put God and Hellenism together and it would work.

Sadducees
Approach: Partner with Rome, especially for material benefit.

Also pro-Hellenism, the Sadducees came from a line of seven priestly families descended from Zadok. Because the Torah stated that the priests were to be in charge, the Israelites put them in charge of the temple and the people after the Maccabean revolt. But within a few decades, they had become completely Hellenistic and corrupt. Not all priests were Sadducees, however. (John the Baptist's father, Zechariah, for example, was a righteous priest but was not a Sadducee.) The Sadducees partnered with Rome, even offering kingship and one of their daughters in marriage to Herod the Great. Eventually, Herod, as King, offered the role of the high priest up to the highest bidder, and Annas, another recognizable name from the Gospels, bought the priesthood from Herod the Great. The Sadducees have been likened to a corrupt religious mafia.

Essenes
Approach: Separate and do not engage.

The Essenes were priests who left because of the corruption of the Sadducees. They moved to the middle of the desert to study and devote themselves to the text. They wanted to know and walk the path of God, believing that if they stayed true to the path, then God would return—and they wanted to be ready. Some of the Essenes continued to serve in the temple, but many of them abandoned the system entirely.

Zealots
Approach: Kill the bad guys.

In a way, the zealots were similar to the Essenes. They rejected Rome and Hellenism, separated themselves, and settled north. However, they were not a priestly group. Instead, they were one of two groups known as the Hasidim, or the "pious ones" in Hebrew. The Zealots were freedom fighters whose zeal was manifested through violence. They were devoted to God but in a violent militant way.

Pharisees
Approach: Get everyone to obey the law.

The second group of the Hasidim, the Pharisees, also had great zeal and passion. They didn't want to separate themselves as the Essenes did, but they did want to create and build a culture of devotion to the Scriptures and Law. They were content to let God deal with Rome while they focused on absolute obedience to God. They believed that when the people of Israel finally were the people God wanted them to be, then God would rescue them and deal with Rome. They viewed the tax collectors, prostitutes, and other sinners as the reason Rome was still in their land. Because sinners were the reason God was not delivering them, they wanted everyone to get in line and obey the Law so God would finally save them.

Each group and each response had its pros and its cons. The Herodians and the Sadducees were perfectly placed for God's mission in the world He wanted to redeem. But they struggled with idolatry—not worshiping the gods of other nations but worshiping the things Hellenism promoted. Leisure, money, comfort, luxury, and self all threatened to remove God from the throne of their hearts.

The Pharisees were devoted to God's Word. Although they were obedient and passionate, many lacked the love and compassion needed to fulfill God's original calling on man. The Essenes were devoted to the text but removed themselves from God's calling by separating from the very world they were to partner with God to redeem. The Zealots also had zeal and passion but believed in redemption through violence.

Holding onto Hope

Each group, in their own way and with their own response, waited for the day the prophets had spoken of when God would come and rescue them from their oppression. They held out hope for the return of God's presence and glory in the rebuilt temple. They also waited expectantly for the Promised Messiah.

- The One whom God promised Adam and Eve at the Fall: "And I will put enmity between you and the woman, and between your offspring and hers; he will crush your head, and you will strike his heel" (Genesis 3:15, NIV).

- The One descended from Abraham through whom all the nations would be blessed. "I will make you into a great nation, and I will bless you; I will make your name great, and you will be a blessing. I will bless those who bless you, and whoever curses you I will curse; and all peoples on earth will be blessed through you" (Genesis 12:2–3, NIV).

- The One from the line of David who would reign forever: "Your house and your kingdom will endure forever before me; your throne will be established forever" (2 Samuel 7:16, NIV).

- The One promised by the prophet Isaiah: "A shoot will come up from the stump of Jesse; from his roots a Branch will bear fruit. The Spirit of the Lord will rest on him—the Spirit of wisdom and of understanding, the Spirit of counsel and of might, the Spirit of the knowledge and fear of the LORD—and He will delight in the fear of the Lord" (Isaiah 11:1–3, NIV).

They waited for the freedom they knew only God could bring. They were not waiting to die to live with God in some other place to escape their oppression. They were waiting for God to return to them and fulfill the promises given to their ancestors. They wanted freedom and liberation in this life, in their communities, families, in this world, and for every generation that would follow.

God's people (and yes, they were still His people), held onto hope with an abundance of expectations.

Chapter 10

Expectancy vs. Expectations

In the morning, LORD, you hear my voice; in the morning
I lay my requests before you and wait expectantly.
—Psalm 5:3, NIV

For to us a child is born, to us a son is given, and the government will be on his shoulders. And he will be called Wonderful Counselor, Mighty God, Everlasting Father, Prince of Peace. Of the greatness of his government and peace there will be no end. He will reign on David's throne and over his kingdom, establishing and upholding it with justice and righteousness from that time on and forever. The zeal of the LORD Almighty will accomplish this.
—Isaiah 9:6–7, NIV

**Have you ever thought about the differ-
ence between living with expectancy and
living with expectations?** Expectancy fills us

with hope, but our expectations can get us into trouble. When we define the anticipated outcome, we begin to believe that only one path—the path we're expecting—can lead to the results we are expecting. We form a picture in our minds of what we want to happen, and too often become so fixated on those expectations that we are unable to see any beauty and wonder outside of them.

There was a time in my life when I felt that God was calling me to take a break from teaching His Word and studying it academically. I had begun *doing* so much for Him that I felt His invitation to move from being a *doer who loves* to a *lover who does*. I responded in obedience and sought intimacy with Him.

During this time, I heard a teacher I admire talk at great length about his intimacy with God—how he heard from Him, how he interacted with Him, and how he served Him. Quite honestly, I became envious of his relationship with God. I wanted that kind of divine intimacy. I also began to pay attention to the people in my life who had the kind of intimacy with the Lord that I desired. I tried to do things the way they did, expecting my intimacy with Him to look the same as theirs. When it didn't, I felt let down by God.

Satan took advantage of the moment, telling me that the kind of intimacy I craved was only meant for certain people—and I wasn't one of them. The liar whispered that I was unworthy of that kind of relationship with the Almighty. But God told me the truth. When I talked to God about my desire and disappointment in prayer, He showed me that my limited expectations had hindered my experience. I had expected God to answer my prayer for closeness in the same way He had for others.

Those expectations had blinded me from seeing all the ways He *had* responded and the ways He had uniquely created me for intimacy. Had I been waiting expectantly rather than with specific expectations, I might have experienced the closeness I desired much sooner.

What God's people wanted—what they expected—was for God to send someone to save them from the oppression of Roman rule. Specifically, the Jewish people believed God was sending a military hero—a liberating, vindicating King—to conquer their current enemy, take the throne, and restore Israel to the abundance and freedom they had experienced under King David.

Had the people of that time lived with expectancy rather than expectations, they might not have limited their vision of what God could do or how He might move. Perhaps by being open to the reality that God moves in ways much bigger than our limited expectations, there wouldn't have been so many who missed God's Promised One when He arrived.

God wanted to change, save, and redeem the culture and every single person in the world.* And yes, He wanted to rescue His people. But because of their expectations, they were hindered. God's chosen people didn't understand that God wasn't sending the Promised One to conquer the Romans. No, He was going after the *real* enemy—the enemy who had started the battle between the kingdoms of God and man at the beginning of time. God's focus wasn't on defeating a political power, but on defeating the source of evil behind human wickedness and injustice, the serpent from the garden, Satan.

God was going to settle this once and for all.

---

*   John 3:16.

Surpassing All Expectation

When the right time came, God sent His Son . . .
—Galatians 4:4a NLT

The Word became flesh and made his dwelling among us.
—John 1:14a, NIV

The long-anticipated time arrived. Immanuel, *God with us*, was born into the world He created. It is stunning to consider that the glory of God which had once filled the Tabernacle and Temple now dwelled in a man. As N.T. Wright explains, "The Son of God, like the tabernacle itself, was a building designed for God Himself to dwell in. The creative Word through whom all things were made came as a human being."[19] The prophecy had been fulfilled, but not in the way God's people expected.

Jesus—Fully God and Fully Man

Jesus Christ, this Promised One, was fully God. Scripture tells us, "He is the radiance of the glory of God and the exact imprint of His nature" (Hebrews 1:3a, ESV).

This time, instead of coming as fire and smoke on a mountaintop or a cloud that filled the Temple, He came as a baby. When Jesus (God with us*) came into the chaotic world in which His people lived, He set aside His divine nature and became *fully* human. It's a mystery we can't completely understand or explain, although we see this truth revealed repeatedly in Scripture. Take it in. The hands that formed mankind from the dust were now the tender hands of an infant.

*   Matthew 1:23

The tiny child was utterly dependent upon the care and love of a family. Can you imagine a greater act of humility and sacrifice?

> *Though he was God, he did not think of equality with God as something to cling to. Instead, he gave up his divine privileges; he took the humble position of a slave and was born as a human being.*
> —Philippians 2:6–7, NLT

> *Since the children have flesh and blood, he too shared in their humanity. . . . For surely it is not angels he helps, but Abraham's descendants. For this reason he had to be made like them, fully human in every way.*
> —Hebrews 2:14a, 16–17a, NIV

As a child, I didn't understand the significance of the full humanity of Jesus. Sunday School and later Bible

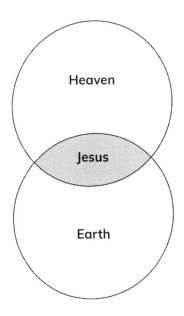

Studies left me wondering why people thought it was such a big deal that Jesus resisted temptation or cast out demons or healed people. I mean, He's God, *right*?

It seemed to me it would not be difficult for God to be *God-like*.

Only later in life did I realize the enormity of the truth that, while Jesus was fully God, He chose to become human.

Fully human.

Jesus came to accomplish what Adam did not: bear the image of God perfectly by living in relationship with God, spreading His light and love, and expanding the Kingdom of God on earth as it is in heaven. A big task for a man who lived with the same limitations, restrictions, and temptations as any other human.

As a man, Jesus could not heal the sick, raise the dead, or cast out demons. But when the time was right, when it was time for His ministry to begin, Jesus went to the Jordan River to be baptized to fulfill the Scriptures He had studied all His life. After His baptism, the heavens opened and the Holy Spirit descended on Him like a dove, and God the Father spoke over Him: "This is my Son, whom I love; with him I am well pleased" (Matthew 3:17, NIV).

With the presence of the Holy Spirit upon Him, Jesus's body became the temple of God—uniting His humanity and the divine nature. As the Tabernacle and Temple had been before, Jesus became a place where Heaven and Earth overlapped.

Empowered by the Holy Spirit, it was time for Jesus to do what the Father sent Him to do. It was time for the Last Adam to defeat Eden's curse and recapture dominion over the earth. It was time for the new Noah to save

God's people from the coming flood of wrath. It was time for all nations to be blessed through Jesus, the seed of Abraham. It was time for the new Moses to give a new law, and for the son of David to take His throne.[20]

Tested in the Wilderness

His work began in the wilderness—and, as with the first Adam, it began with a choice. Matthew tells us the reason for His camping trip in the desert: "Then Jesus was led up by the Spirit into the wilderness to be tempted by the devil" (Matthew 4:1, ESV). Jesus seems to have known there would be a test, and He prepared for it by fasting for forty days and forty nights. We know that in Scripture, the spiritual practice of fasting is not simply about depriving oneself but about strengthening one's connection to God and is always accompanied by prayer. For forty days and forty nights, Jesus spent time with His Father, fortifying Himself with truth and love.

Being fully human, at the end of that time of fasting, Jesus was hungry. He surely would have felt physically weak. Which, of course, is when Satan chose to attack. He saw an opportunity to potentially thwart God's plan for the Promised One and Anointed One before it could go any further.

Satan understood that the kingdom of man—his domain—was at risk. Jesus had come to reclaim the authority Adam and Eve had given away and to build God's Kingdom. Attempting to trick Jesus the same way he had God's first image bearers, Satan offered Jesus a shortcut.

The devil led him up to a high place and showed Him in an instant all the kingdoms of the world. And he said to him, "I will give you all their authority and splendor; **it has been given to me, and I can give it to anyone I want to.** *If you worship me, it will all be yours.*

—Luke 4:5–7, NIV

(emphasis added)

Satan knew and even admitted to Jesus that the power he was using to influence the world (the kingdom of man) had been given to him. He offered it to Jesus, *if* Jesus, as Adam and Eve had, would choose to listen to him instead of God.

The first Adam failed to subdue the serpent by choosing to believe the lie and obey the deceiver. Jesus, the Last Adam, made a better choice—the perfect choice. Knowing God's Word, understanding God's character, and trusting in God's goodness and plan, Jesus resisted the devil. He refused to buy into his twisted words and promises and instead silenced his lies with the truth of God.

Bringing the Kingdom of Heaven to Earth

Having passed that test in the wilderness, Jesus's ministry launched in full force. Everywhere He went, He told people the good news about the Kingdom of God.

"The time promised by God has come at last!" he announced. "The Kingdom of God is near! Repent of your sins and believe the Good News!"

—Mark 1:15, NLT

A new kingdom was coming! And as the perfect image bearer, Jesus modeled what it looked like when God was in charge. He brought order to chaos by diffusing hatred with love, caring for the poor, and seeking the downtrodden. He healed the sick, raised the dead, cleansed lepers, and cast out demons. He prayed for His enemies, went the second mile, and turned the other cheek. He brought God's redemptive solution into every encounter, bringing the reality of heaven into the earth. And He did it through love and self-sacrifice, "For even the Son of Man did not come to be served, but to serve, and to give his life as a ransom for many" (Mark 10:45, NIV).

For Heaven and Earth were being joined, and the kingdom was expanding every time Jesus brought in God's love and power. N.T. Wright says,

> When Jesus healed people, when he celebrated parties with all and sundry, when he offered forgiveness freely to people as if he were replacing the Temple itself with his own work—in all these ways it was clear, and he intended it to be clear, that this wasn't just a foretaste of a future reality. This was reality itself. This was what it looked like when God was in charge. God's kingdom was coming as he taught His followers to pray, "on earth as in heaven . . ." God was already becoming king in the new way he had promised. It was happening, and this is what it would look like.[21]

The last Adam—Jesus—executed God's original plan, given in the garden, and fought against the real enemy of God's people. The battle and the Promised One were different from what they expected, but this victory set God's people free and established His rule forever.

God's people are to be liberated, the battle is to be won, not by force of arms but by a different power, the power that John's Gospel most accurately describes: love.

> *Having loved his own who were in the world, Jesus*
> *loved them to the end.*
> —John 13:1, NIV

The Perfect Sacrifice

Jesus fought and won the battle against the origins of evil, corruption, and death by taking on death itself as the perfect sacrifice. He fulfilled the promise of forgiveness of sins that God made when He cut covenant with Abraham and walked through the blood path on Abraham's behalf.

Since the establishment of the Tabernacle, priests blew the *shofar* (a hollowed ram's horn) every day at 9:00 a.m. and 3:00 p.m. The sound of the *shofar* coming from the Temple reminded the people of God's promise to their father, Abraham. Twice daily, the people stopped what they were doing to observe a moment of silence. While a priest was offering a sacrifice and throwing blood on the Temple's altar, the people's hearts cried out to God, "Remember your promise!"

And then, on a Passover Friday, almost 1,800 years after God cut covenant with Abraham, Jesus hung on a cross. At 3:00 p.m., just as it had every day for centuries, the shofar blew. In the Temple, an animal was sacrificed

---

All at once and for all time, Jesus's perfect sacrifice gave humanity direct access to God.

---

once again. On the cross, Jesus raised his head and screamed, "It is finished!" His blood dripped onto the sand, paying for our sins once and for all.

He was pierced for our transgressions, he was crushed for our iniquities; the punishment that brought us peace was on him, and by his wounds we are healed. We all, like sheep, have gone astray, each of us has turned to our own way; and the LORD has laid on him the iniquity of us all.
—Isaiah 53:5–6, NIV

The earth shook when, with His final words, Jesus gave up His Spirit. N.T. Wright points us back to creation to explain the meaning of this promise-keeping, world-altering moment: "The echo is of Genesis: at the end of the sixth day, God completed all the work that he had done. The point was not to rescue people from creation but to rescue creation itself. With the death of Jesus, that work is complete. Now, and only now, and only in this way can new creation come about."[22]

The Temple curtain that for centuries had symbolized the separation of a holy God from a sinful people was ripped from top to bottom. All at once and for all time, Jesus's perfect sacrifice gave humanity direct access to God.

Therefore, brothers and sisters, since we have confidence to enter the Most Holy Place by the blood of Jesus, by a new and living way opened for us through the curtain, that is, his body . . . let us draw near to God with a sincere heart and with the full assurance that faith brings. . . .
—Hebrews 10:19–20, 22, NIV

G.K. Beale says in *God Dwells Among Us*, "The embroidery on the temple veil represented the starry heavens of the old cosmos. Consequently, the tearing of the curtain suggests symbolically the tearing and the beginning of the destruction of the old world, as the presence of God breaks out from the Holy of Holies and begins to create a new world."[23]

Jesus was the Lamb of God who gave His life to take away the sins of the world. He took on the full weight of evil so the new world could be born. "Jesus was speaking and acting in such a way as to imply that he was to go ahead of his people, to meet the powers of destruction in person, to take their full weight on himself, so as to make a way through, a way in which God's people could be renewed, [and] could rediscover their vocation to be a light to the nations. . . ."[24]

Jesus–Defeating Death, Bringing Life Eternal

But Christ has indeed been raised from the dead, the firstfruits of those who have fallen asleep.
—1 Corinthians 15:20, NIV

Death could not hold Jesus, and three days later, He rose from the dead. With His resurrection, Jesus reclaimed the authority Adam and Eve had forfeited. "And having disarmed the powers and authorities, he made a public spectacle of them, triumphing over them by the cross" (Colossians 2:15, NIV). From that moment of disobedience in the garden, Satan used the power he had deceitfully won to dominate the world. But when Jesus defeated death, He defeated the serpent. And He told

His disciples, "All authority in heaven and on earth has been given to me" (Matthew 28:18, NIV).

Jesus's resurrection marked the beginning of a new world with God as King.

Here's the Good News: Jesus Is *Alive.*

Through Jesus's life, death, and resurrection, Satan, sin, and death have been defeated.

Since the children have flesh and blood, he too shared in their humanity so that by his death he might break the power of him who holds the power of death- that is, the devil- and free those who all their lives were held in slavery by their fear of death.
—Hebrews 2:14-15, NIV

Because of His perfect sacrifice, we are forgiven, saved, and redeemed.

If you openly declare that Jesus is Lord and believe in your heart that God raised him from the dead, you will be saved. For it is by believing in your heart that you are made right with God, and it is by openly declaring your faith that you are saved.
—Romans 10:9–10, NLT

Praise be to the God and Father of our Lord Jesus Christ, who has blessed us in the heavenly realms with every spiritual blessing in Christ. In him we have redemption through his blood, the forgiveness of sins, in accordance with the riches of God's grace that he lavished on us.
—Ephesians 1:3,7–8a, NIV

> *For he has rescued us from the dominion of darkness*
> *and brought us into the kingdom of the Son he loves,*
> *in whom we have redemption, the forgiveness of sins.*
> —Colossians 1:13–14, NIV

We have direct access to God and can approach the throne boldly.

> *Therefore, brothers and sisters, since we have confidence to enter the Most Holy Place by the blood of Jesus, by a new and living way opened for us through the curtain, that is, his body, and since we have a great priest over the house of God, let us draw near to God with a sincere heart and with the full assurance that faith brings.*
> —Hebrews 10:19–22a, NIV

> *Let us then approach God's throne of grace with confidence, so that we may receive mercy and find grace to help us in our time of need.*
> —Hebrews 4:16, NIV

That's good news, indeed! But the good news does not stop there. For many years, I believed that Jesus's death and resurrection simply granted us the chance to leave this world and spend eternity in heaven someday. But there is so much more to the story.

And we have a role to play in it.

Restoration

Chapter 11

God's Plan for the Church

*But you are a chosen people, a royal priesthood, a
holy nation, God's special possession, that you may
declare the praises of Him who called you out of
darkness into His wonderful light.*
—1 Peter 2:9, NIV

*Repent and be baptized, every one of you, in the
name of Jesus Christ for the forgiveness of your
sins. And you will receive the gift of the Holy
Spirit.*
—Acts 2:38, NIV

**I never had the chance to know my mom's
father, but I treasure the stories she and
Mom-Mom (my grandmother) shared
about him through the years.**
They both had a few of his belongings that I loved
to look at as I imagined what my grandfather must have
been like. One of these items was an old Ford Model A.

God's plan and purpose was, and still is, established in love.

As a child of the 1970s, I can still remember the first time I saw that 1920s-era car. Complete with a rumble seat, it was nothing like the station wagon I was used to riding around in! That antique car delighted me, even though it looked every bit of its old age—rusted, the original color no longer visible, broken door handles, and worn out everything. At one time, the car had functioned perfectly, but after decades of enduring the elements and disuse, it no longer ran. I suppose my mom could have chosen to get rid of it; after all, it was only a shell of what it had been. Instead, my dad and great-uncle decided that rather than discard it, they would restore it.

Together, they spent almost every Saturday for several years rebuilding and restoring that old Model A. When they were done, the car looked brand new! It had been brought back to its original color, the engine had been rebuilt, and all the broken pieces had been fixed. In 1992, my dad drove it in our hometown parade. Once again, the car was able to do what it had been made to do. It had been restored, renewed. And it was beautiful.

God has similar plans for all of creation. And it will be beautiful.

N.T. Wright notes that "Jesus's kingdom project is nothing if not the rescue and renewal of God's creation project."[25] God's plan and purpose was, and still is, established in love. Because He is intensely and fundamentally relational, God created mankind for relationship. Then He built a home, a cosmic temple in which to live with them. He gave His image bearers the task of expanding His kingdom until it filled the whole earth with a culture defined and blessed by God's goodness and love.

Adam and Eve's choice to sin separated God and man and derailed His creation project. God's love, however, is too great to be stopped. He began again with Noah, then with Abraham, then with Israel, then finally, He took on flesh and came to the world He created. Through the perfect sacrifice of Jesus, His Son, He brought reconciliation and *reinstated His original plan*, because as N.T. Wright puts it, "The power that has tyrannized the old creation has been broken, defeated, overthrown. God's Kingdom is now launched, and launched in power and glory, on earth as in heaven. New creation has begun; and its *motivating power is love*."[26]

With the restoration of authority, it was time for God's original plan, in this new creation, to get back on track, and for His people to pick up the original call of humanity.

God's Expansion Plan

While on earth, Jesus brought God's light into the world through His words and actions, demonstrating what it looked like when God was in charge. He gathered His own *talmidim* or disciples. For three years these disciples followed their Rabbi and learned how great the Father's love was for them personally and for humanity as a whole. They learned at their Master's feet and through His example. They discovered that by loving others, they were demonstrating their love for the Father. And as they grew in faith and understanding, those closest to Jesus joined His mission to announce and demonstrate the coming Kingdom of God.

After his death and resurrection, and before ascending into heaven, Jesus told His *talmidim* that now *they* were to continue the mission. It was their turn to take the lead in expanding God's Kingdom until it covered the world. They would do that by doing everything they had watched Jesus their Rabbi do for the years they had been with Him.

> *Then Jesus came to them and said, "All authority in heaven and on earth has been given to me. Therefore go and make disciples of all nations, baptizing them in the name of the Father and of the Son and of the Holy Spirit, and teaching them to obey everything I have commanded you."*
> —Matthew 28:18–20a, NIV

His directions were clear. The original calling had not changed since the beginning of time. His salvation and goodness and love were not meant for only a few to experience. He was after the entire world. Jesus directed those who'd had front row seats to what it looked like when the power of heaven came to earth to spread out and fill creation with His goodness. Empowered by the Holy Spirit, they were to bring peace to chaos, order to disorder, love to hate, the Kingdom of Heaven to Earth.

It was, no doubt, a big task and an important calling. Which is why Jesus promised they wouldn't have to do it alone or in their own power. They just had to wait for the Promised Helper to arrive.

You will receive power when the Holy Spirit has come upon you and you will be my witnesses in Jerusalem, in all Judea and Samaria, and to the ends of the earth.
—Acts 1:8 NIV

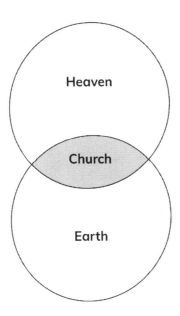

A New Fire

When God's presence filled both the Tabernacle and the Temple in Old Testament times, a great cloud of smoke overwhelmed the space. When Moses met with God on top of Mount Sinai, he did so by entering the cloud that rested on the mountain, and Scripture tells us, "To the Israelites the glory of the LORD looked like a consuming fire on top of the mountain" (Exodus 24:17, NIV).

Fifty days after Jesus's resurrection, that fire was back. With a violent wind and a roaring noise, the Promised Helper—God's Holy Spirit—descended from Heaven.* Just as the heavens opened and the Holy Spirit descended on Jesus at His baptism, anointing Him and filling Him with power, tongues of fire descended from Heaven and came to rest upon Jesus's followers, filling them with the Holy Spirit. At that moment, everything changed for Jesus's followers:

- The same Spirit who empowered Jesus to spread God's Kingdom and bring a redemptive solution to the world now dwelled in them, enabling them to do everything they had seen Jesus do and accomplish the calling originally given to Adam and Eve in the garden.

- With the indwelling of the Holy Spirit, every believer of Jesus, which collectively came to be known as the church, became—as Eden, Mount Sinai, the Tabernacle, the Temple, and Jesus had been—a place where Heaven and Earth intersected. They carried the very presence and authority of God with them into every encounter and space.

N.T. Wright explains the union this way:

> *With Jesus joining heaven and earth together in his own person, the Holy Spirit, which anointed and equipped Jesus himself for his kingdom work, comes pouring out onto his followers. . . . Where they are, heaven and earth are joined together. Jesus is with them, his life is at work in and through them, and they are the place where the living God, the God who*

---

*   Acts 2:1–4

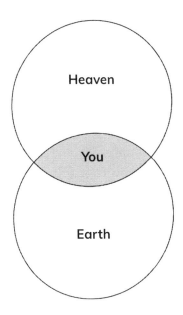

is reclaiming the world for his own, is alive and active and establishing his sovereign rule. . . . Now the new Temple—Jesus and his Spirit-filled followers—is the place from which and through which God is beginning to implement the world-transforming kingdom that was achieved in and through Jesus and his death and resurrection.[27]

Let's not gloss over this truth: Every single person who confesses Jesus as Lord, as a place where Heaven and Earth overlap, carries the presence of God and the kingdom *wherever* they go. They are the ones through whom God is reclaiming the world for His own and bringing Restoration!

Do we matter in the story of God? Do we have a role to play? More than we can even imagine.

Here's the Good News: God is with you, here and now.

After Jesus exhorted His disciples to go into all the nations, He ended with this promise, "And surely I am with you always, to the very end of the age" (Matthew 28:20, NIV). That promise remains true for us today. We can be sure that Jesus is powerfully present with and in us. Through the presence of the Spirit, we are guided and directed and enabled to make His sovereign rule a reality. Because Jesus never taught His followers how to escape the mess of the world. "He was training them to be kingdom bringers."[28] He was training them to be a part of His Restoration plan.

You, dear reader, are to be a "kingdom bringer." Remember, with the Holy Spirit in you, you are a place where Heaven and Earth overlap.

You are a place where people come into contact with the life and power of Heaven. You are empowered and equipped as a royal priest to bring God's Kingdom on Earth and declare His glory. For in the Holy Spirit, "a new power is let loose in the world, the power to remake what was broken, to heal what was diseased, to restore what was lost."[29]

In our role as royal priests, we aren't meant to just wait for a future hope—we are filled with the Holy Spirit so that we can bring God's hope everywhere we go and expose and undo the works of our enemy.

When we understand this, our knowledge of Jesus becomes more than the reality of Him as our Savior; He is also our model. We seek to learn from Him and *follow His example*. In fact, Jesus said, "Whoever believes in me will do the works I have been doing, and they will do *even greater things* than these, because I am going to the Father" (John 14:12b, NIV, emphasis added).

We are called to make a difference in this world, not just wait for another world or reality to appear. Jesus died to make us redeemed and restored image-bearers with a role to play in God's purposes for the world. How? I'm glad you asked. We'll cover that next.

Chapter 12

Holding on to Hope

The Church Age

I pray that the eyes of your heart may be enlightened in order that you may know the hope to which he has called you, the riches of his glorious inheritance in his holy people, and his incomparably great power for us who believe. That power is the same as the mighty strength he exerted when he raised Christ from the dead and seated him at his right hand in the heavenly realms, far above all rule and authority, power and dominion, and every name that is invoked, not only in the present age but also in the one to come.
—Ephesians 1:18–21, NIV

And God raised us up with Christ and seated us with him in the heavenly realms in Christ Jesus . . .
—Ephesians 2:6, NIV

> *Since, then, you have been raised with Christ, set*
> *your hearts on things above, where Christ is, seated*
> *at the right hand of God. Set your minds on things*
> *above, not on earthly things. For you died, and your*
> *life is now hidden with Christ in God.*
> —Colossians 3:1–3, NIV

Imagine that you are at your favorite coffee shop. As you're reading and enjoying your London Fog, a friend sits down beside you. You glance up and see a troubled look on her face.

Clearly hurting, she says, *I know Jesus died to save me from my sins. I know that because of His death and resurrection, I will live with Him for eternity. I also know that through His death and resurrection, God has become King. Jesus is Lord, right now. But I am struggling in this world full of hardship, death, persecution, and pain. It's not enough for me to feel secure about my eternity—how is the gospel supposed to affect how I live today? What can I do right now?*

I battle with the same "What can I do *right now*" question every day. Let's face it: life is messy. At times, it feels unbearably heavy. As I am writing this, I have a friend who lost her niece weeks before she was going to graduate high school, a family member whose cancer has come back and is ravaging her body, several friends who are worried about children who have walked away from their faith, and a friend who has suffered great abuse from a trusted family friend. Four weeks before I got to this chapter, I learned that my dad only has a few months to a year to live. And I haven't even mentioned what we see on the news each day. I could go on and on describing the hardships and heartache facing humanity, and I know you could add to my list. Heaviness and darkness seem to cover this world.

Alongside *Star Wars*, the *Lord of the Rings* trilogy is a favorite of mine. (If you aren't familiar with the story or aren't into fantasy, bear with me.) In the story, an unimaginable evil is increasing in power and influence on Middle Earth. The people in that world are filled with despair because of the strength behind such reckless hate and the visible successes of darkness and evil. Two of the main characters in the story are hobbits (an imaginary race known for their small size), Frodo and Sam.

At the end of the second movie, Frodo and Sam are both burdened by the weight of their mission to rid the world of evil. They are discouraged by the multiple losses they've experienced. In despair, Frodo turns to Sam, ready to give up:

Frodo: "I can't do this, Sam."

Sam: "I know. It's all wrong. By rights, we shouldn't even *be here. But we are.*

"It's like in the great stories, Mr. Frodo. The ones that really mattered. Full of darkness and danger, they were, and sometimes you didn't want to know the end. Because how could the end be happy? How could the world go back to the way it was when so much bad happened?

"But in the end, it's only a passing thing, this shadow. Even darkness must pass. A new day will come. And when the sun shines, it will shine out the clearer.

"Those were the stories that stayed with you. That meant something. Even if you were too small to understand why.

"But I think, Mr. Frodo, I do understand. I know now. Folk in those stories had lots of chances of turning back, only they didn't. Because they were holding on to something."

Frodo: "What are we holding on to, Sam?"

Sam: "That there's some good in this world, Mr. Frodo. And it's worth fighting for."[30]

Frodo and Sam's boldness and courage never fail to inspire me. Being the weakest and the smallest of the races, they could have excused themselves from the fight. But instead, they stood firm and persevered despite all odds, setbacks, and losses. And, holding onto hope, they pressed on. That choice led to victory for the entire Middle Earth.

What are you holding on to?

The world today feels wrong because it is. The evil around us is not what God purposed. The injustice, abuse, oppression, misuse of authority, disease, violence, poverty—none of that is God's intention or desire for what was once a "very good" creation. His heart grieves over the havoc wreaked by what sin brought into the world.

The world today feels wrong because it is. The evil around us is not what God purposed.

The truth is that a spiritual battle wages all around us. Like Frodo, sometimes we feel in our hearts that we don't have the strength to go on. It can seem as if the darkness is winning, and we are powerless against it. But in this time and place that God ordained for our lives, we too face a choice. Are we going to trust God? Will we, with the *chutzpah* of Abraham and Moses, hold on to the hope that our God is a covenant-making, covenant-keeping God who will redeem and restore all things? Or not?

Will we choose to shine God's light into the dark places to expand His kingdom? Or will we trust what is seen rather than unseen and succumb to the kingdom of man?

Fear can tempt us to cower as victims, biding our time as if we are powerless. But we are far from powerless. We know the end of the story, and because of Christ, we are victors. With the big picture in view, we can, as Sam told Frodo, believe that the world is worth fighting for and that we have a role to play in sharing the hope and light of Jesus with the world. Jesus, who, *"for the joy set before him,* endured the cross, scorning its shame, and sat down at the right hand at the throne of God"* — is our model.

We are called, as believers, as victors in Jesus, for the joy set before *us* to not grow weary or lose heart. We know that by the cross and resurrection, the ultimate battle has already been won. But the truth remains: We live in the pages between the books of Jude and when Jesus returns (because He is coming back!). The kingdom *is here*, and the kingdom *is to come*. The victory has been assured but not yet fully realized. Death is defeated, yet we still see and feel death every day. Just as the Israelites waited for 400 years between the Old Testament and Christ's birth, we are in a season of waiting.

---

*   Hebrews 12:2b, NIV

What do we do while we wait?

We live out our calling.

The original call on mankind given in the Eden temple remains: We are to be the *imago dei*, God's image bearers, reflecting who God is to the world, ruling and reigning in partnership with Him. With the authority and dominion Jesus won at Calvary, we have the power to accomplish this calling while we hold the tension between the "already and not yet" of the Kingdom of God.

We have the divinely inspired Word of God to wield as a weapon, *just as Jesus did in the wilderness*. When the enemy comes at us with his lies, taunts us with doubts, and tries to distract us from our calling, we banish him with Scripture. When Satan whispers lies that target our greatest fears, we can stand and declare God's truth as our own:

> *Greater is He who is in me*
> *than He who is in the world.*
> —1 John 4:4

> *Satan, you are a conquered enemy, powerless over me.*
> —Colossians 2:15

> *I am not a victim of your schemes or anything the world would throw at me, but I am a **powerful victor** in Jesus Christ. And today I choose to stand unswervingly in the truth that I am fully loved by God and that His divine power has given me everything I need for life and godliness.*
> —2 Peter 1:3

We have the armor of God we can put on daily to stand firm in prayer against the devil and the powers of evil we will encounter as we seek to do God's work.

> *Finally, be strong in the LORD and in his mighty power. Put on the full armor of God, so that you can take your stand against the devil's schemes. For our struggle is not against flesh and blood, but against the rulers, against the authorities, against the powers of this dark world and against the spiritual forces of evil in the heavenly realms. Therefore put on the full armor of God, so that when the day of evil comes, you may be able to stand your ground, and after you have done everything, to stand. Stand firm then, with the belt of truth buckled around your waist, with the breastplate of righteousness in place, and with your feet fitted with the readiness that comes from the gospel of peace. In addition to all this, take up the shield of faith, with which you can extinguish all the flaming arrows of the evil one. Take the helmet of salvation and the sword of the Spirit, which is the word of God.*
>
> —Ephesians 6:10–17, NIV

Truly, we have everything we need in Jesus Christ and the power of the Spirit to expand the Kingdom of Heaven on Earth. What does the Kingdom of God, that His image bearers are meant to expand, look like?

Like one overflowing with the power of love.

Follow the Way

Jesus was the perfect **role model.** He demonstrated the best way to approach the world in which we live. Notice that Jesus's approach was not to "go along and get along," "to seek one's own interest at the expense of others," "to separate from the world and not engage," "to use redemptive violence," or even "to *make* everyone obey the Law."

Jesus took a holy and wholly different approach which He summed up with two commands:

> *"'Love the Lord your God with all your heart and with all your soul and with all your mind.' This is the first and greatest commandment. And the second is like it: 'Love your neighbor as yourself.' All the Law and the Prophets hang on these two commandments."*
> —Matthew 22:37–40, NIV

We want to be people of zeal and passion, but we must remember that, above all, we are called to be people who love.

> *"By this everyone will know that you are my disciples, if you love one another."*
> —John 13:35, NIV

Just as Moses taught the Israelites a new way to live, **Jesus showed us, the church, how to live.** The Beatitudes and the Sermon on the Mount* detail the way kingdom people are to live and think. We demonstrate God's love by following our Savior's teachings. When we read that the Kingdom of Heaven belongs to us—those who recognize our only hope is in Jesus and that He is worth everything we are and have to offer—it does not just mean we will go to Heaven when we die. It means that we will be one of those through whom God's Kingdom, the rule of Heaven, begins to appear on Earth.

---

*　　　Matthew 5–7

Jesus demonstrated God's love and now calls us to do the same. We don't seek to follow the rules to earn favor from God but to *challenge radically the way the world does things by living differently.* By demonstrating God's love through our actions and words, we show the world what it looks like when God is in charge.

We, like Jesus, are to diffuse hatred with love, care for the poor, and comfort the downtrodden. We, through the power of the Holy Spirit in us—the same power God used when He raised Jesus from the dead—are to heal the sick, raise the dead, cleanse the lepers, and cast out demons. We are to pray for our enemies, go the second mile, feed the hungry, turn the other cheek, and rescue lost sheep. We are to expose and undo the works of the enemy, right what wrongs we can right, and bring God's redemptive solution into every encounter. We are not to be overcome by evil but to overcome evil with good!* We are to fight against the darkness, appropriating the power given to us. Because Christ and His sacrifice and what He accomplished is worth fighting for.

Jesus is with us *always*, so we seek to emulate Him in *all* things. With God as our King, we must be willing to take risks as we learn to release the power of God that dwells in us into the circumstances of life. We are a host of God himself. There is no greater privilege, and there is no greater responsibility. As a place where Heaven and Earth overlap, and with the presence of God within us, we owe the world an encounter with the risen Jesus!

---

*   Romans 12:21

Kingdom Living in the Real World

What does all this look like in practice? In truth, as image bearers, we can show and share God's love in countless ways, both big and small—although nothing is small when it comes to God's Kingdom! He has a way of multiplying our efforts when we seek to serve Him by loving others.

Sometimes, though, other people's examples can inspire us or help us notice opportunities we may have missed, so I wanted to share just a few ways I've seen people working to expand God's Kingdom.

In my hometown, a former pastor founded a ministry to help people who are taking steps toward self-sufficiency but need a vehicle. The ministry, OnRamp, finds reliable vehicles for them (through gifts, donations, or purchases) and services them for the first year free of charge. Since 2017, OnRamp has helped more than one hundred families by providing them with cars.

A woman I know spends hours each week visiting nursing homes. She simply sits and listens to residents' stories.

A group of friends pulled together to pay the medical bills for another friend who was receiving treatment for cancer.

When a couple with newborn twin boys was struggling financially, a friend and her family bought the twins' diapers for their first year.

A man I know makes sure he knows the name of each person he talks to, whether it is at the grocery store, a restaurant, or the movies. He wants those he encounters to know that they are seen and valued.

I have a dear friend who was assaulted on a cruise

in her early twenties. The violent experience rocked her world and challenged her view of God. Dear friends, mentors, and family gathered around her and spoke to her grief. They took her to a private gym and told her that while she may have no hope, they were holding hope for her. They spent hours with her as she released her physical energy, providing her with a safe place where she could process her hurt and grieve all she had lost. They checked in with her regularly, never letting her be alone for too long. By walking with her through the healing process, they demonstrated the love of Jesus.

It all matters. A gentle word, a smile, a kindness, a financial donation, the gift of time volunteering—every act of love expands God's Kingdom. We live out our calling person by person, prayer by prayer, moment by moment.

A Path Marked with Suffering

As we seek to do what Jesus did, we are faced with the truth that Jesus's path to kingship was unlike any other. Unlike earthly kings and rulers, Jesus didn't barrel into the world, obliterating the enemy by military force. To the puzzlement of many, His path involved suffering, misunderstanding, violence, and eventually, execution.

In bringing many sons and daughters to glory, it was fitting that God, for whom and through whom everything exists, should make the pioneer of their salvation [Jesus] perfect through what he suffered.
—Hebrews 2:10, NIV

As we seek to enforce the victory obtained at Calvary, we will experience hardship. Jesus won his victory by suffering, and the same will be true for many of His followers. We see this clearly in the suffering of the saints throughout the New Testament and in the lives of many since the beginning of the church.

Now if we are children, then we are heirs—heirs of God and co-heirs with Christ, if indeed we share in his sufferings in order that we may also share in his glory.
—Romans 8:17, NIV

N.T. Wright says, "The Spirit and suffering. Great joy and great cost. Those who follow Jesus and claim him (and proclaim him) as Lord learn both of them. It's as simple as that."[31] As much as we would like life to be easy once we choose to follow Jesus, it just doesn't work that way. But our hope enables us to stand and face the troubles of this world because we know that we are overcomers because of the blood of the Lamb and by the word of our testimony.*

Here's the Good News: Jesus has overcome the world.

In Jesus, we can hold on to God's truth and promises with *chutzpah*! Jesus gave His life so that we will live with Him in eternity, but He is also good news for our lives *today*. No matter what we see, experience, or read about, we know that Jesus has overcome the world. He tells us this plainly in John 16:33. Jesus says, "I have told you these things, so that in me you may have peace. In this world you will have trouble. But take heart! I have overcome the world."** Even if we feel the darkness is getting the last word, we know that in the end, it will not.

---

*   Revelation 12:11
**   John 16:33, NIV

We have what we need. Suffering and temptation will come, but God gives us the grace, power, and way to overcome every trial as we seek to fulfill our mission in His kingdom.

And God is faithful. He will not allow the temptation to be more than you can stand. When you are tempted, he will show you a way out so that you can endure.
—1 Corinthians 10:13b NLT

We are not alone. The temptations in our lives are no different from what others experience. They are no different from what Jesus experienced. Being fully man and fully God, Jesus understands the struggles we face and is right beside us as we walk through them.

Because he himself suffered when he was tempted, he is able to help those who are being tempted.
—Hebrews 2:18, NIV

Our suffering makes an eternal difference. When we respond to suffering or to challenging circumstances by trusting God, our example can embolden, encourage, or invite people into God's Kingdom.

We do not lose heart. Though outwardly we are wasting away, yet inwardly we are being renewed day by day. For our light and momentary troubles are achieving for us an eternal glory that far outweighs them all.
—2 Corinthians 4:16-17, NIV

Jesus prays for us. Before He went to the cross, Jesus prayed that you would have the kind of unity He shared with God and the Holy Spirit. Today, Jesus continues to pray for you by name.

> *Christ Jesus who died—more than that, who was raised to life—is at the right hand of God and is also interceding for us.*
> —Romans 8:34b, NIV

God will never fail or forsake us. God is faithful and unchanging. His love never fails.

> *For God has said, "I will never fail you. I will never abandon you."*
> —Hebrews 13:5b, NLT

Jesus will return and all things will be set right. The hardships we face are temporary. The sorrow we feel will one day be replaced with eternal joy and peace.

> *Behold, He is coming with the clouds, and every eye will see Him, even those who pierced Him; and all the tribes of the earth will mourn over Him. So, it is to be. Amen.*
> —Revelation 1:7, NASB

Chapter 13

The Kingdom to Come

Growing up in church, I heard a lot about what I was saved from. I was saved *from* sin. Saved *from* hell. What I didn't hear much about was what I was saved *for*, except that when I died there was this place "up there" I would go called Heaven, where I would be with My Savior for all eternity. In fact, I repeatedly heard, spoke, and found comfort in the phrase, "This earth is not my home." Imagine my surprise when I came to understand that in truth, earth *is* my forever home. Heaven is not where I will spend eternity.

Consider this: The reason people die today and go to Heaven is because of sin. Michael E. Wittmer explains in *Heaven is a Place on Earth*, "If Adam and Eve had never sinned, they would have continued to live on this planet, enjoying the beauty of creation as they walked in close fellowship with their Creator."[32] But Adam did sin, and his sin brought death into the world. One of the consequences of sin, Wittmer notes is that, "all people must die—an event that separates their souls from their bodies. Their bodies immediately begin to decay, but their souls continue to live."[33]

Today, when believers die, their souls go to Heaven. But what is not often understood or taught is that those in Heaven have not yet achieved their perfect state. The Heaven we think of now is not the Heaven of eternity. Believers who die join the saints who have gone before them and are now in the presence of God, but it is not our ultimate end to "bow before God as a disembodied soul."

Even before Adam and Eve sinned, God had a rescue plan. Throughout Scripture, we see God working to get "the people of God in the place of God in the presence of God" as He rescues, redeems, and restores. That is why we are told in Revelation that the eternal Heaven is not some place "up there" that we will go to escape Earth. Instead, we read that Heaven will come down to Earth where they will be united for all time, and God will dwell with man for all eternity, just as He planned.

The New Heaven and New Earth

Then I saw a new heaven and a new earth, for the old heaven and the old earth had disappeared... And I saw the holy city, the new Jerusalem, coming down from God out of heaven like a bride beautifully dressed for her husband. I heard a loud shout from the throne saying, "Look, God's home is now among his people! He will live with them, and they will be

his people. God himself will be with them. He will wipe every tear from their eyes, and there will be no more death or sorrow or crying or pain. All these things are gone forever."
—Revelation 21:1–4, NLT

As Wittmer says, "Our departure from this world is just the first leg of a journey that is round-trip."[34] Our souls will not remain forever with God in Heaven, but God will bring Heaven down to earth where He will live with us forever, and our departed souls will reunite with our resurrected bodies.

Okay, stop. Read that again: *Our departed souls will reunite with our resurrected bodies.* Something I never learned in vacation Bible school or youth camp. In fact, in discussing this with my eighty-year-old mother who has gone to church all her life, she said to me, "Are you kidding me?" She had missed this truth too!

But Paul talks about this clearly in 1 Corinthians 15. It is a very long and complex chapter, but I encourage you to take time to read each word and chew on this passage.

But tell me this—since we preach that Christ rose from the dead, why are some of you saying there will be no resurrection of the dead? For if there is no resurrection of the dead, then Christ has not been raised either. And if Christ has not been raised, then all our preaching is useless, and your faith is useless. And we apostles would all be lying about God—for we have said that God raised Christ from the grave. But that can't be true if there is no resurrection of the dead. And if there is no resurrection of the dead, then Christ has not been raised. And if Christ has not been raised, then your faith is useless and you are still guilty of your sins. In that case, all who have died believing in Christ are lost! And if our hope in Christ is only for this life, we are more to be pitied than anyone in the world.

But in fact, Christ has been raised from the dead. He is the first of a great harvest of all who have died.

So you see, just as death came into the world through a man, now the resurrection from the dead has begun through another man. Just as everyone dies because we all belong to Adam, everyone who belongs to Christ will be given new life. But there is an order to this resurrection: Christ was raised as the first of the harvest; then all who belong to Christ will be raised when he comes back.

But someone may ask, "How will the dead be raised? What kind of bodies will they have?" What a foolish question! When you put a seed into the ground, it doesn't grow into a plant unless it dies first. It is the same way with the resurrection of the dead. Our earthly bodies are planted in the ground when we die, but they will be raised to live forever. Our bodies are buried in brokenness, but they will be raised in glory. They are buried in weakness, but they will be raised in strength. They are buried as natural human bodies, but they will be raised as spiritual bodies.

What comes first is the natural body, then the spiritual body comes later. Adam, the first man, was made from the dust of the earth, while Christ, the second man, came from heaven. Just as we are now like the earthly man, we will someday be like the heavenly man.

What I am saying, dear brothers and sisters, is that our physical bodies cannot inherit the Kingdom of God. These dying bodies cannot inherit what will last forever.

But let me reveal to you a wonderful secret. We will not all die, but we will all be transformed! It will happen in a moment, in the blink of an eye, when the last trumpet is blown. For when the trumpet sounds, those who have died will be raised to live forever. And we who are living will also be transformed. For our dying bodies must be transformed into bodies that will never die; our mortal bodies must be transformed into immortal bodies.

Then, when our dying bodies have been transformed into bodies that will never die, this Scripture will be fulfilled:

> *Death is swallowed up in victory.*
> *O death, where is your victory?*
> *O death, where is your sting?*
> —I Corinthians 15:12–23, 35–36, 42–44,
> 46–47, 49–55, NLT

Our current bodies—mortal, decaying—cannot exist in the eternal New Heaven and New Earth. But that doesn't mean that we won't have bodies. Instead, what it means is that our bodies will be different—glorified! The dead will be raised and changed.

Just as Jesus went through death and was resurrected in a transformed physical existence, we, in hope, wait for the same. The risen Jesus had a physical body that others could touch. He ate food and drank wine as he talked with His followers. He had scars on His hands and feet. He was the same Jesus they had followed

before His death, and in a way we don't really understand, He was also different. He could appear and disappear from rooms. Not everyone recognized Him at
first. We can't fully understand or explain it, but we
know, as John says:

> *We are already God's children, but he has not yet
> shown us what we will be like when Christ appears.
> But we do know that we will be like him, for we will
> see him as he really is.*
> —1 John 3:2, NLT

It's a mystery—but our old body will become a
new body, transformed. What do we do in light of this
knowledge? Paul provides an answer to that question:

> *Therefore, my dear brothers and sisters, stand firm.
> Let nothing move you. Always give yourselves fully
> to the work of the Lord, because you know that your
> labor in the Lord is not in vain.*
> —1 Corinthians 15:58, NIV

A Global Restoration Project

We are not the only ones who look forward to the day
when our bodies will be free from death and decay.
Paul tells us in Romans that creation is also longing for
that day:

> *Yet what we suffer now is nothing compared to the
> glory he will reveal to us later. For all creation is
> waiting eagerly for that future day when God will
> reveal who his children really are. Against its will,
> all creation was subjected to God's curse. **But with
> eager hope, the creation looks forward to the***

*day when it will join God's children in glorious freedom from death and decay. For we know that all creation has been groaning as in the pains of childbirth right up to the present time. And we believers also groan, even though we have the Holy Spirit within us as a foretaste of future glory, for we long for our bodies to be released from sin and suffering. We, too, wait with eager hope for the day when God will give us our full rights as his adopted children, **including the new bodies he has promised us**.*

—Romans 8:18–23, NLT

(emphasis added)

Tim Mackie notes,

> At this moment, the earth is cut off from the full life of heaven. I don't think we have to look too far before we can confirm this by mere observation: crime, inequality, rampant greed, and selfishness. To use a biblical metaphor, creation groans like a woman in childbirth. But the new creation is here, taking form even when we can't see it. We do sense hints of it now and then, though, just like we might make out an elbow or foot poking from within a pregnant woman's belly. One day it will be pushed forth into life, like a new baby emerging from the womb.[35]

But isn't the earth going to be destroyed by fire? That is a common belief among many; in fact, it's what I was taught as a child. However, many scholars disagree with this assumption. I, too, have a hard time believing that the earth will be annihilated because God is a God who redeems and restores. God will accomplish what He has planned. He always does. We've seen that throughout Scripture.

The confusion is understandable, however, when you see verses, like 2 Peter 3:7 (NIV), which says "the present heavens and earth are reserved for fire," or 2 Peter 3:10 (NIV): "the heavens will disappear with a roar; the elements will be destroyed by fire, and the earth and everything done in it will be laid bare."

That sounds like ultimate destruction, right? But many theologians believe that in verse seven, Peter is writing about the fire of judgment, not the fire of destruction. And in using the words "will be laid bare" in verse ten, he is offering the picture of a refiner's fire.

When metal is refined, it is thrown into a fire where eventually soil, impure elements, and unwanted minerals rise to the surface and are sloughed off. When the process is complete, the refiner can look into it and see his image. The metal—gold, silver—is pure and appears in perfect beauty.

In the same way, the earth will be refined: All the impurities will be purged until we are left with a redeemed and restored creation. The fire is a purging, not an annihilating fire. In fact, Peter compares the destruction of fire to the previous destruction by water in 1 Peter:

> *By these waters also the world of that time was deluged and destroyed. By the same word the present heavens and earth are reserved for fire, being kept for the day of judgment and destruction of the ungodly.*
> — 1 Peter 3:6–7, NIV

The flood did not destroy the world but cleansed it. In the same way, the impending fire will do the same.

As Wittmer says, "If the 'destruction' of the flood did not annihilate the world, why should we think that the future 'destruction' by fire will do so?"[36]

God created the physical universe to glorify Him. And He created mankind with their physical bodies to bear His image. God is not a God who backs out on His plan. It makes sense, then, that He will redeem all of creation and clothe us with immortality because His Son paid the price of His life so that God could be glorified in our bodies forever and ever.

For you know that it was not with perishable things such as silver or gold that you were redeemed from the empty way of life handed down to you from your ancestors, but with the precious blood of Christ, a lamb without blemish or defect.
—1 Peter 1:18–19, NIV

There will be a day when we will live and work with God on this redeemed earth, just as He planned at creation. After all, work was something mankind was made to do (Genesis 2:15), for in itself, work is not a curse. It was, in fact, a part of the "very good" earth before the Fall and was only made difficult after sin was welcomed into the world. But just imagine what it will be like in the new heaven and new earth without the stress, frustration, pain, difficulty, and conflict between sinners that we currently experience. Imagine everyone fully free to use their God-given gifts to create and build a culture with God at the center!

What will the redeemed and restored world be like? I can't even begin to fully understand, much less explain it. But I do know it will be like this current world but without sin. Think of all the beauty we find in nature,

> *Just imagine what it will be like in the New Heaven and New Earth without the stress, frustration, pain, difficulty, and conflict we currently experience.*

art, business, and music. Think of the trees, waterfalls, rivers, birds, and animals—they will all be there, a home where redeemed humans will live forever with God.

The story of Scripture is the story of Immanuel, God with us: God with us in the garden, God with us in the wilderness, God with us in flesh, and God with us in the person of the Holy Spirit, until, as written by John.

> I heard a loud shout from the throne, saying, "Look, God's home is now among his people! He will live with them, and they will be his people. God himself will be with them. He will wipe every tear from their eyes, and there will be no more death or sorrow or crying or pain. All these things are gone forever."
>
> And the one sitting on the throne said, "Look, I am making everything new!" And then he said to me, "Write this down, for what I tell you is trustworthy and true." And he also said, "It is finished! I am the Alpha and the Omega—the Beginning and the End. To all who are thirsty I will give freely from the springs of the water of life. All who are victorious

will inherit all these blessings, and I will be their God, and they will be my children.
—Revelation 21:3–7, NLT

And just as all of life started in a garden, it returns to a garden.

Then the angel showed me a river with the water of life, clear as crystal, flowing from the throne of God and of the Lamb. It flowed down the center of the main street. On each side of the river grew a tree of life, bearing twelve crops of fruit, with a fresh crop each month. The leaves were used for medicine to heal the nations.

No longer will there be a curse upon anything. For the throne of God and of the Lamb will be there, and his servants will worship him. And they will see his face, and his name will be written on their foreheads. And there will be no night there—no need for lamps or sun—for the Lord God will shine on them. And they will reign forever and ever.
—Revelation 22:1–5, NLT

Here we have a new Eden where John saw the tree of life, accessible to all and eternally bearing fruit because its roots extended to the river of life. This river of life will, as Tim Mackie says, "dispense nourishment to all the new creation because it flows from the presence of God Himself. However, in John's account of a garden, humanity wasn't represented by a couple. John describes seeing all the nations there, working to cultivate the garden as Adam and Eve did in Genesis. He saw that the fulfillment of God's purpose through Jesus would result in the restoration of humans to their place as co-rulers of God's world, ready to work with God to take creation into uncharted territory. But it's not just a return back to the garden; it's a step forward into a new Jerusalem, a great city where human cultures and all their diversity work together in peace and harmony before God."[37] Can you even imagine?

This is the hope we have when we understand *the whole story*:

> God's domain and our domain will one day completely unite. All things will be made new. Death will be replaced with life. The whole earth will be a recreation of the garden, and the glory of the temple will cover it. Every nation will be blessed through the power of the resurrected Jesus, and God's own personal presence will permeate every square inch of the new creation.[38]

Amen and Amen. Thank you, Jesus.

We are able to hold unswervingly to our full gospel hope because we know, as Sam answered Frodo:

> "But in the end, it's only a passing thing, this shadow.
>
> Even darkness must pass.
>
> **A new day will come.**
>
> And when the sun shines, it will shine out the clearer."

The Hope of Knowing the *Whole Story*

Jesus's life, death, and resurrection saved you from your sins so you can live with Him for eternity. Until then, you are an image bearer, a temple, a royal priest, part of a kingdom of priests. You are a place where Heaven and Earth intersect. By the power of the Holy Spirit, you are equipped and empowered to bring light into the darkness, peace into chaos, expand the borders of the garden, and work to bring the Kingdom of Heaven to Earth. You do not only wait for a future hope, but you are also a vessel who brings God's hope everywhere you go. One day Jesus will return and you will reign with God on this redeemed earth in your glorified body, along with believers who have gone before you, and who will join you after.

These truths cannot be shaken, no matter what is going on around you or within you. These truths fuel a light within that the darkness cannot overcome. These truths cause fear to disappear and be replaced with a confident expectation in the character and love of your God, who did so much to bring you back into His arms forever.

Chapter 14

Are You Ready to Live Unhindered?

Now the Lord is the Spirit, and where the Spirit of the Lord is, there is freedom.
—2 Corinthians 3:17, NIV

So if the Son sets you free, you will be free indeed.
—John 8:36, NIV

Before we left the hospital to take our firstborn, Abby, home, a nurse came to my room to see if I had any questions. Boy, did I! I babysat before, sure, but I had never been *the provider* for another life, especially one so tiny and precious. I asked that poor nurse question after question about how to feed Abby, bathe her, and help her sleep, and I took copious notes. I couldn't believe the doctor was just going to let my husband and me take this fragile, teeny newborn home without any supervision! The responsibility of caring for this sweet gift weighed heavily on me—like a thick and dreadful darkness. (Shout out to Abram!) *I was scared out of my mind.*

Whenever I feel confused, worried, or don't know what to do, my habit is to buy a book. You can imagine how my library grew during those first few years of Abby's life. I had a plethora of books about babies, from newborns to toddlers. Each book gave great information on the cognitive development of children at her age, as well as general advice for common toddler issues. What I couldn't find, and the resource I really wanted, was a book that offered step-by-step instructions for handling specific issues, such as what to do when your child climbs out of her crib at eighteen months, refuses to eat, refuses to nap, will not listen, throws a tantrum in Target, flips out in church because her red crayon dropped on the sloping floor and rolled out of her reach, and so on. If I had a question, I wanted a book to answer it specifically.

I've often felt that way in my walk as a Christian. I've attended women's events, for example, where I nodded and said "amen" along with the speakers, totally bought into the messages they shared, only to leave with excitement but no understanding of how to apply the truths I had just heard. I want the *how*, preferably in three simple steps.

Because of that aspect of my personality, I wish this final chapter could tie everything up with a big bow. I'd love to give you a step-by-step guide on how to live unhindered and free in the light of the whole story. But here's the truth: Life doesn't follow a formula. The details of your circumstances and struggles are different from mine. None of us knows what our next day, much less the next month, holds.

I also wish I could go through the life-toppling experiences I shared in the first chapter and tell you each one has been resolved, everyone is happy, and there are no more problems. But life and humans are too messy for that to be true. Here's what happened.

We ended up changing churches, and I still carry the scars from the pain of our experience. To this day, I must intentionally fight feelings of cynicism and fear when it comes to investing more of myself in church ministry. But I have trusted friends who call me out when I let fear dominate. Along with the Holy Spirit, they lovingly encourage me to keep taking steps forward. And I do my best to listen.

My husband eventually stopped traveling for work, and we learned how to communicate and partner together again. Repairing our relationship required intentionality and diligence. Right now, our relationship is strong, and we have agreed to never stop working toward greater unity in preparation for each new stage of life.

It was many, many months before my friend and I talked about the break in our relationship. I am not exaggerating when I say that it was one of the most painful things I have gone through. It was made even harder by the fact that we had overlapping circles, and although we barely made eye contact, I saw her quite frequently. One day, I wrote her name on a piece of paper, put it in a jar, and then placed the jar on the highest shelf in my house as a picture of me giving the whole situation to God. I knew I could do nothing more to restore this dear relationship. Eventually, she contacted me and we went to breakfast. Since then, we have had several discussions and have grieved together over the loss. We have not, however, returned to the closeness we once shared. But God, in his faithfulness and kindness, strengthened other relationships and surrounded me with new friends during that time. As I worked through the pain, He brought healing to my heart, enabling me to trust and invest in those new friendships and receive the beauty they continue to bring. More than ever, I am learning how to let God love me. I am learning that my identity is in Him and who He says I am. I still occasionally slip into unhealthy thought patterns and have to be intentional in catching and reminding myself of what God's Word says. I post Scripture all over my house (even laminated in my shower) and in my car as a way to replace ungodly beliefs and Satan's lies with the truth.

I have come to be okay with the truth that my walk with the Lord is a process. Each day, I learn more and become even braver. Each day, I grow. I never do things perfectly and never will. But I know I have everything I need through my heavenly Father who made me and loves me as I am. I am also forever grateful that we can truly never blow it. He is always there, ready to forgive and restore.

Years ago, as I was beginning to learn and process all that I've written about in this book, the Lord gave me three words—words I felt He wanted me to keep in mind: radiant, rooted, and unhindered. While there is no formula for life, these three words have helped me better understand God and His love, as expressed throughout His whole story. They also shape the way I see myself in His story.

I hope sharing them with you will give you a similar blessing.

Radiant

For God, who said, "Let light shine out of darkness," made his light shine in our hearts to give us the light of the knowledge of God's glory displayed in the face of Christ.
—2 Corinthians 4:6, NIV

The phrase *imago dei* and what it means radically changed my understanding of my life's purpose. It means that, as God's image-bearers, through the power of the Holy Spirit, we are to reflect who God is to the world around us. Our role is to expand the Kingdom of Heaven here on Earth by shining His light into the dark places. In other words, we are called to be radiant.

How do we radiate the light of God? We find the answer in Psalm 34:5, NIV:

*Those who look to him are **radiant** . . .*
(emphasis added)

Being radiant is a result of our focus on God and our heart's alignment with His.

I have a dear friend who, before she enters any store or restaurant, will ask God, "How do you want me to shine your light in here?" or "What are your thoughts and words for this waiter who is serving us?" She listens for the prompting of the Holy Spirit and then shares what He puts on her heart with the person God highlights for her. Sure, some people have thought she was crazy, but more times than not, it has blessed the life of the recipient. Her intentionality to look to God and to share Him with others is her way of shining His light on those she encounters.

> I am the **light of the world**. *Whoever follows me will never walk in darkness, but will have the* **light of life.**
> —John 8:12b, NIV
> (emphasis added)

What if we walked in the truth that we have the light of life? What if we asked God to reveal to us how we can shine His light regularly? What if we did what He asked? The answer is plain:

> You are the light of the world. . . . **let your light shine** *before others, that they may see your good deeds and* **glorify your Father in heaven.**
> —Matthew 5:14a, 16, NIV
> (emphasis added)

When we look to God and follow Him, the way we live attracts others to *Him*. We dispel the darkness as we become more like Him, which allows others to see God for who He is.

> *In him was life, and that life was the light of all mankind. The light shines in the darkness, and the darkness has not overcome it.*
> —John 1:4–5, NIV

We have a choice, just as Adam and Eve and the Israelites did. Are we going to be overwhelmed by the darkness we see in the world today, or are we going to be overwhelmed by our God—who He is, what He has done, and what He is going to do? No matter how dark the world may seem on any given day, the truth remains: The darkness cannot overcome the light of the truth of the glory of God.

Perhaps you grew up singing "This Little Light of Mine," believing that your light was, indeed, little. But, friend, when you are reflecting the Light of the world, you are radiant. There is nothing small or inconsequential about that.

Rooted

As good as our hearts and intentions may be, I'll be the first to admit that it is difficult to keep our calling to be radiant before us day after day. The dulling minutiae of life, like when someone cuts you off in traffic or you keep getting transferred to person after person when you're making a call regarding your insurance, can make you feel less than shiny. How do we consistently shine the light of Christ? We must root ourselves daily.

One day when I was pumping gas, God revealed to me how easy it is to treat Him and His Word like a gas station. We get caught up in the busyness of life, topping off our tanks with a quick prayer or devotional reading when we can, until we find ourselves running on empty.

Knowing the only way to become full again, we finally set aside time to immerse ourselves in Scripture and prayer. After several days of doing this, we feel a shift in our hearts and minds that only time with God can bring. Full, once again, we return to the busyness of life, and our times with God get shorter. Until we're empty again.

Certainly, God welcomes us anytime we come to Him. He is always faithful to give us what we need. However, treating Him like a gas station does not enable us to bear fruit that lasts. And that is the call on our lives. After all, Jesus said:

> *You did not choose me, but I chose you and appointed you so that you might go and bear fruit—**fruit that will last**.*
> —John 15:16a, NIV
> (emphasis added)

Being radiant is a fruit that comes out of being *rooted*. Jesus shared this with His disciples:

> *Abide in me, and I in you. As the branch cannot bear fruit by itself, unless it abides in the vine, neither can you, unless you abide in me.*
> —John 15:4, ESV

Abide. Root yourself in Jesus. That's where we find the nourishment that enables us to bear fruit—to be radiant.

Read what Banning Liebscher writes in his book, *Rooted: The Hidden Places Where God Develops You*:

> In the growth cycle of fruit-bearing plants, fruit comes at the very end. The cycle starts with a seed being planted in the ground. When watered, the seed will break open and begin to put down roots. That root system will continue to grow as the seed forms a shoot and eventually breaks through the surface of

the soil into air and sunlight. Both the plant and its root system will keep growing until the plant is strong and mature enough to bear fruit. Significantly, in order for a plant to survive, much less bear fruit, its root system has to take up more space underground than the plant takes up above ground. When you look up at one of those immense redwoods in the Avenue of the Giants, for example, you're actually standing on root systems that are wider than those trees are tall. This is the principle of foundations. A foundation always has to be bigger than the thing it is supporting.

Fruitfulness in your life comes about through a similar process. God plants the seed of His word inside you (see Luke 8:11) and waters it with His Holy Spirit, bringing it to life. He begins to give you insight into who He created you to be in Him and what He is calling you to do with Him. He stirs up that desire in you to have a lasting impact in the world. And then He starts to build a root system for that seed in your heart, your internal world.

Your heart is your point of connection with Jesus—the place where you become rooted in your relationship with Him. He wants to develop His heart to heart connection with you to the point where you become fully united with Him, where you think like He thinks, want what He wants, speak like He speaks, and do what he does. This is what it means to remain in Him. Only when you remain in Him will you produce fruit that lasts.

For you to bear abundant, enduring fruit, God needs to make you bigger on the inside than you are on the outside. You have to let Him build your root *system in secret before He leads you into making a visible impact in the world.*[39]

We must be rooted in order to fulfill our purpose and the calling God has on our lives. Practically speaking, how do we do this?

We root ourselves in Scripture.

Jesus is not only our Savior (again, as absolutely wonderful as that is); He is also our model and Rabbi. As His disciples, we are to follow Him. But in order to follow Him, we must see where He is going. We must come to really know Him. And along with prayer, the place to do that is in the Bible. The Bible reveals Jesus and contains His teachings. God gave us His Word for us to seek Him and find Him. God's Word is to be the foundation of our lives.

> *Blessed is the one*
> *who does not walk in step with the wicked*
> *or stand in the way that sinners take*
> *or sit in the company of mockers,*
> *but **whose delight is in the law of the Lord,***
> ***and who meditates on his law day and night.***
> *That person is like a tree planted by streams of*
> *water, which yields its fruit in season*
> *and whose leaf does not wither—*
> *whatever they do prospers*
> —Psalm 1:1–3, NIV
> (emphasis added)

We must be students of God's Word. We must be able to distinguish truth from lies and the Word of God from the voice of the world.

Specifically, Psalm 1 tells us we are to delight and meditate on the Word. These adjectives describe something beyond simply reading. To have deep roots, we must go deep into Scripture—studying it, memorizing it, contemplating it, praying it, *doing* it—just as the One we follow did.

I once heard a teacher compare meditating on Scripture to a raisin. We can pop a raisin in our mouths, chew it, and enjoy it. But we can also pop a raisin in our mouths and let it sit there for a while. Eventually the raisin rehydrates because of the moisture in our mouths. Then, when we bite into it, the raisin is even sweeter. There is great benefit to reading the Scriptures every time you can. But the Word is even sweeter when you remain in it, study it, meditate on it. And when we do, we are like trees planted by water.

> *Blessed is the one who trusts in the LORD,*
> *whose confidence is in him.*
> *They will be like a tree planted by the water*
> *that sends out its roots by the stream.*
>
> *It does not fear when heat comes;*
> *its leaves are always green.*
> *It has no worries in a year of drought*
> *and never fails to bear fruit.*
> —Jeremiah 17:7–8, NIV

We root ourselves in His love.

As I write this, although I am forty-nine years old, I vividly remember the pain of rejection faced as a college freshman. I had dreamed of joining a particular sorority ever since I was a little girl. My mother was a former vice-president of the group. She had shared stories and for years, I'd seen the group on campus when we attended the annual homecoming games. It felt like part of my family history, and I never considered the idea of not being accepted into this group.

The night before I was to learn whether I had been accepted, an old college friend of my mom, who was the alumni advisor of that group, phoned to tell her that I had been rejected. The reason? The sorority wasn't looking for girls from the less-desirable, industrialized section of Houston, nor did they want a girl who had a little extra meat on her bones. I'd like to tell you that I brushed off the rejection and said, "their loss." But I didn't. Instead, I let their decision define my worth. I struggled *for years,* bearing the weight of not being good enough.

I imagine we all have stories like that, which run deep. Experiences that have caused us to battle against the lies of the enemy and the world that seeks to define our value and identity in things that, honestly, have nothing to do with our worth. But God's love can heal all our wounds, from those like I experienced in college to those that are unspeakably evil, which occurred at the hands of others.

My friend, there is always hope. God makes all things new. When we are rooted in Jesus and in His Word, we come to understand and *truly believe* that our worth is determined by Him, and Him alone. As the *imago dei,* created by the Almighty God because He desired a relationship with us, we are loved more than we can even imagine. All the loves of the world pale in comparison to His. By remaining in Him and in the Word of God, we root ourselves in God's love.

I like to take the following Scripture and turn it into a prayer for myself and for others:

I fall to my knees and pray to the Father, the Creator of everything in heaven and on earth. I pray that from his glorious, unlimited resources he will empower you with inner strength through his Spirit. Then Christ will make his home in your hearts as you trust in him. Your roots will grow down into God's love and keep you strong. And may you have the power to understand, as all God's people should, how wide, how long, how high, and how deep his love is. May you experience the love of Christ, though it is too great to understand fully. Then you will be made complete with all the fullness of life and power that comes from God. Now all glory to God, who is able, through his mighty power at work within us, to accomplish infinitely more than we might ask or think.

—Ephesians 3:14–20, NLT

We root ourselves in community.

Confession: This one does not always come naturally to me. I am an introvert who doesn't mind being alone. I recharge that way. I also have a tendency to withdraw when I am going through really tough seasons. I like to hunker down and just make my way through. I have learned through experience, however, that Satan *wants* me to isolate myself when I am suffering. When I withdraw into myself, I play right into his hands.

There is a God-given level of protection available in a believing community. When we let others speak into our lives and help and comfort us in our times of trial, we receive the love of God as well as their support.

When we go to church and sing and worship, even when we don't feel like it, we hear and declare truths that stand against lies that threaten to take root in our hearts. When we serve others, we focus on them instead of our own stuff. And that is good.

I mentioned earlier that I received terrible news about my father's health not too long ago. The heartbreak made me want to crawl into bed and stay there for days. I even thought about canceling plans to attend a retreat where I had agreed to serve. My dad's illness seemed like a good enough reason to bow out. The event's leaders were gracious and told me to do whatever was best for my family and myself. As I prayed about it, I realized that while what I wanted to do was to stay home and wallow, what I needed was to go and serve at this retreat, to interact with others, and to have the opportunity to declare God's truth to them and pray over them.

I went. And in sharing in this gift of community, God stirred my faith and ministered to me deeply through my sisters there.

Let us think of ways to motivate one another to acts of love and good works. And let us not neglect our meeting together, as some people do, but encourage one another, especially now that the day of his return is drawing near.
—Hebrews 10:24–25, NLT

Two people are better off than one, for they can help each other succeed. If one person falls, the other can reach out and help. But someone who falls alone is in real trouble. Likewise, two people lying close

together can keep each other warm. But how can one be warm alone? A person standing alone can be attacked and defeated, but two can stand back-to-back and conquer. Three are even better, for a triple-braided cord is not easily broken.
—Ecclesiastes 4:9–12, NLT

Did you know that during Hurricane Katrina in 2005, only four out of over 700 oak trees died? Curious about this, home builders looked into why this was the case because you'd see pictures of great devastation, but there in the middle of the rubble would be oak trees, leaves still on, standing.

What they discovered is that the oaks were able to remain standing because, under the ground, an oak tree's roots are entwined with the root of the oak trees next to it. When a hurricane hits, it's not hitting one tree but a whole community.

When we are in community, we do not suffer a single attack from the world or from the enemy alone. When we root ourselves in community, worshiping together, serving together, and growing together, our roots grow deep together. And together we are able to withstand whatever storm may come our way.

Unhindered

This brings us to living unhindered.

Perhaps it's easy to grasp the concepts of and callings to be radiant and rooted. But how can we be rooted *and* simultaneously unhindered? It seems like a contradiction in thought. But we know freedom is a promise and truth of the gospel. Scripture even makes it sound like a command.

It is for freedom that Christ has set us free. Stand firm, then, and do not let yourselves be burdened again by a yoke of slavery.
—Galatians 5:1, NIV

. . . let us throw off everything that hinders and the sin that so easily entangles. And let us run with perseverance the race marked out for us, fixing our eyes on Jesus, the pioneer and perfecter of faith.
—Hebrews 12:1–2a, NIV

The burdens we bear come in many forms. Some are thrust upon us, and some we voluntarily pick up. Others are things we've been carrying for so long because we thought we had to, were expected to, or because we believed that's just the way life is. Some burdens are the sins we hide and refuse to give up because they feel normal or comfortable. Other burdens started out as good intentions that turned into legalistic musts. Rather than drawing us into closer relationship with God, they push us into transactional religion.

It can seem impossible to live unhindered when everything, from the tedious, day-to-day life stuff to the heart-wrenching sorrows, seems to pile on one after the other, weighing us down. Anxiety, stress, pain, inadequacy, depression, regret, shame—you may have other words to add to the list of feelings and circumstances that hinder you from living out your calling to be a radiant image-bearer of God. Those same feelings and circumstances may make you feel less like you're rooted and more like you're trapped.

But that is not the desire God has for you. Jesus offers something different, something better.

*Come to me, all you who are weary and burdened,
and I will give you rest. Take my yoke upon you and
learn from me, for I am gentle and humble in heart,
and you will find rest for your souls. For my yoke is
easy and my burden is light.*
—Matthew 11:28–30, NIV

Come to Me.
Find rest.
Be unburdened.
Live *unhindered.*

Let's go back to David's words in Psalm 34:5: *Those
who look to him are radiant.* Consider the words on either
side of this promise and notice how the concepts of
radiant, rooted, and unhindered work together:

*I sought the LORD, and he answered me;
he delivered me from all my fears.
Those who look to him are radiant;
their faces are never covered with shame.
This poor man called, and the LORD heard him;
he saved him out of all his troubles.*
—Psalm 34:4–6, NIV

Rooted

David rooted himself in his relationship with God. He
knew God's love, His holiness, His promises, and his
ability to save because he meditated on God's Word.
(Read Psalm 119 and count the times David uses the
word meditate.) David soaked in and soaked up all that
God offered him. Did he still face hardship? Clearly.
Did he still sin? Absolutely. But his life was not defined
by the things that he could have allowed to weigh him
down. It was defined by the One to whom he looked.

The same will be true for you when you grow those roots down deep into God's Word and your relationship with God the Father, Jesus the Son, and the Holy Spirit. With the indwelling power of God's Spirit, you can stand tall and secure when the storms of life hit. And they will. But when you are rooted in Him, you are saved by Him. Because Jesus defeated death when He rose from the grave and took back the authority that Adam and Eve had relinquished to Satan, you are victorious.

Radiant

Looking to God is what makes us radiant. Remember how Moses's face literally shone when he was in God's presence? When we look to God, we can't help but radiate His goodness and shine His light into the world. That is what we were created to do, after all.

Unhindered

But look at what else we find in this passage: freedom. God delivers. He saves. He frees us from shame. Both in a physical and spiritual sense, God is the One who empowers us to live *unhindered*. When you are rooted in God and radiantly display the *imago dei*, you have the power to fight *from* victory, not for it. Victory is already yours! But victory over what? Over anything that tries to hold you back or weighs you down: fear, anxiety, depression, shame, self-doubt and the need for others' approval, procrastination, perfectionism, and sin. Because of God's love, the saving grace of Jesus, and by the power of His Holy Spirit living in you, you are free, blameless, righteous—*unhindered*—not just someday but right here, now, today, in this life.

*Therefore, there is now no condemnation for those
who are in Christ Jesus, because through Christ
Jesus the law of the Spirit who gives life has set you
free from the law of sin and death.*
—Romans 8:1–2, NIV

That, my friend, is the good news.

My prayer for you is that you will live in that freedom today and always as you fulfill your calling as the *imago dei* and an ambassador of Christ, sharing the *whole story*.

Acknowledgments

I fell in love with books at a very young age (Thank you, Mom and Dad!) and dreamed of being an author one day. However, as life went on, that dream was buried. So much so that I no longer even considered working to make it come true. It is only because of the many cheerleaders God has placed in my life that the dream resurfaced and became a reality.

I have the biggest champion in my husband, Josh. Thank you for always encouraging me to race after the desires God has put in my heart and not letting me skip over the ones that scare me. I am incredibly grateful for the ways you have challenged me to examine my unhealthy views of God and introduced me to the truth that God is intensely and fundamentally relational. From the very beginning of this journey, you have encouraged me every step of the way, never complaining about my writing retreats or the extra tasks that were added to your schedule as a result. I am so thankful for you and our shared love and passion for the story of God.

My kids—Abby, Ellie, Jonathan, and Jacob—thank you for believing in me and encouraging me always. Ellie, I don't know how many times you prodded me by asking, "When are you going to write your book?"

Thank you for reminding me of my dream and not letting me let it go.

To my mom, Mary, and my dad, Jeff—this would not be a reality without the two of you. Mom, thank you for introducing me to Jesus and modeling His love every day. Dad, thank you for passing down your love for learning all things scriptural! And both of you—for your support and for believing in me my whole life— thank you.

Kevin Still—I can't adequately put into words how much I appreciate your guidance in the whole writing process. You calmed me down when I freaked out and helped me put a plan in place to make this happen. You held me accountable and faithfully read chapter after chapter multiple times. Thanks for believing in me.

Shauna Maness—From the first time you heard me teach on the full gospel, you have encouraged me with your belief in this message. I don't know how many hours you have spent poring over version after version of each chapter and offering great insight and ideas. Thank you.

Michelle Dew—Would this book have even happened without our many trips and writing retreats? Thanks for pushing me and lifting me up out of my own head when I doubted. Thank you to the Dew family for the use of your ranch to get away and focus on writing. The same goes for my brother and sister-in-law, Jeffery and Charity, and the use of your beautiful hill-country home!

Thank you to Angela Robinson for cheering me on, helping me tighten the message, designing the images, and adding clarity—along with a million other things! Your gift of friendship is priceless.

Erin Casey and the publishing team—thank you for helping turn my dream into a reality.

McKenna Ryan—you make beautiful things. Thank you for all your design work. You have a gift! Thanks for sharing it with me.

Michelle Thomas and Melissa Darst—your nudges and belief in me were so perfectly timed and played a key role in me choosing to sit down and finally get to writing.

Leah Sequeira—my friend, mentor, and coach. God works powerfully in my life through you. I don't believe I'd be where I am without your guidance and love.

My roundtable discussion group—Chris White, Brian Lee, Leah Sequeira, Joan Quintana, Jamie Bomnskie, Ashley Brusenhan, Christy Willhite, and Denise Hagen. Your input was invaluable. Thank you, Jamie Suel, for reading in the midst of all the ways you serve. Time is one of the biggest gifts you can give, and I am humbled that all of you gave of yours so willingly.

Thank you to Stephanie Lee, Ashley Brusenhan, and the You Are team, as well as Lauren Vassar and the Unknown Tour for the opportunities to share this message that God has given me. I am beyond honored by your trust. I am forever grateful and love linking arms with you for the advancement of God's Kingdom!

I am supported by so many amazing friends and family members—many who read advanced copies, voted on possible titles, sent me encouraging texts, inquired how things were going, and spoke life into me all during the process. I do not take that lightly. To the hot honeys, besties, and Kosta girls, I love you. My life is stronger and richer because of each one of you.

I am overwhelmingly grateful for my community of Christ-followers who live what they believe, expanding the borders of the garden, ushering in the Kingdom of Heaven on Earth now. I learn from you. *You encourage me.*

It is my prayer that this book offering honors all those who have sown into me and, most importantly, our Father, God.

Resources

The Epic of Eden: A Christian Entry into the Old Testament by Sandra L. Richter

How God Became King: The Forgotten Story of the Gospels by N.T. Wright

Simply Jesus: A New Vision of Who He Was, What He Did, and Why He Matters by N.T. Wright

A New Heaven and a New Earth: Reclaiming Biblical Eschatology by J. Richard Middleton

God Dwells Among Us: Expanding Eden to the Ends of the Earth by G.K. Beale and Mitchell Kim

The Temple and the Church's Mission: A Biblical Theology of the Dwelling Place of God by G.K. Beale

The Day the Revolution Began: Reconsidering the Meaning of Jesus's Crucifixion by N.T. Wright

Surprised by Hope: Rethinking Heaven, the Resurrection, and the Mission of the Church by N.T. Wright

The King Jesus Gospel: The Original Good News Revisited by Scot McKnight

The Lost World of Genesis One: Ancient Cosmology and the Origins Debate by John H. Walton

The Bible Project Podcast

The Bema Podcast

Endnotes

1   Middleton, J.R., "The Ancient Universe and the Cosmic Temple," *BioLogos*. July 19, 2016. https://biologos.org/series/evolution-and-biblical-faith-reflections-by-theologian-j-richard-middleton/articles/the-ancient-universe-and-the-cosmic-temple.

2   Laurence, Trevor. "The Temple of Creation: Part One," *Cateclesia.com*. July 15, 2020. https://cateclesia.com/2020/07/15/the-temple-of-creation-part-one.

3   Gage, Warren Austin. *The Gospel of Genesis: Studies in Protology and Eschatology.* Winona Lake, IN: Carpenter Books, 1984.

4   "Temple Study Notes," *Bible Project.* https://d1bsmz3sdihplr.cloudfront.net/media/Study%20Notes/Temple_Study-Notes.pdf.

5   N.T. Wright, *Simply Jesus: A New Vision of Who He Was, What He Did, and Why He Matters.* New York, NY: HarperCollins, 2012.

6   Walton, John H. *The Lost World of Genesis One: Ancient Cosmology and the Origins of Biblical Religion.* Downers Grove, IL: InterVarsity Press, 2011.

7   Middleton, J.R. "The Ancient Universe."

8   Walton, John H. *The Lost World.*

9   Richter, Sarah L. *Epic of Eden.*

10   Middleton, Richard. *The Liberating Image: The Imago Dei in Genesis 1:26–27 and the Human Condition.* Grand Rapids, MI: Brazos Press, 2005.

11 Richter, Sarah L. *Epic of Eden.*

12 Fohrman, David. *The Beat that Crouches at the Door: Adam & Eve, Cain & Abel, and Beyond.* New Milford, CT: Devora, 2007.

13 Ibid.

14 Walton, John H. *The Lost World of Adam and Eve.*

15 Richter, Sarah L. *Epic of Eden.*

16 Tyson, Jon. *Beautiful Resistance: The Joy of Conviction in a Culture of Compromise.* Colorado Springs, CO: Multnomah, 2020.

17 Ibid.

18 Wright, N.T. *The Day the Revolution Began: Reconsidering the Meaning of Jesus's Crucifixion.* New York, NY: HarperCollins, 2016.

19 Wright, N.T. *The Day the Revolution Began*

20 Richter, Sarah L. *Epic of Eden.*

21 Wright, N.T. *Simply Jesus.*

22 Ibid.

23 Beale, G.K. and Mitchell Kim. *God Dwells Among Us: Expanding Eden to the Ends of the Earth* (Downers Grove, IL: InterVarsity Press, 2014).

24 Wright, N.T. *Simply Jesus.*

25 Ibid.

26 Ibid. (emphasis added)

27 Ibid.

28 Ibid.

29 Ibid.

30 Jackson, Peter. 2002. *The Lord of the Rings: The Two Towers.* United States: New Line Cinema.

31 Wright, N.T. *Simply Jesus.*

32   Wittmer, Michael E. *Heaven is a Place on Earth: Why Everything You Do Matters to God.* Grand Rapids, Michigan: Zondervan, 2004.

33   Ibid.

34   Ibid.

35   Mackie, Tim. "The New Heaven and New Earth as Depicted in Revelation 21-22." *The Bible Project.* https://bibleproject.com/articles/new-heaven-new-earth.

36   Ibid.

37   Ibid.

38   Ibid.

39   Liebscher, Banning. *Rooted: The Hidden Places Where God Develops You.* New York, NY: Waterbrook, 2016.

40   Richter, Sarah L. *Epic of Eden*

About the Author

Meredith Perryman is passionate about equipping believers to grab hold of their identity and inheritance in Christ. Her heart is to use Scripture to inspire and empower people to walk unhindered in truth for the advancement of God's Kingdom. She lives out her purpose by teaching and coaching women and speaking at ministry events across the country.

After serving as the teaching director of a local Community Bible Study (CBS) women's class for many years, Meredith has taken her life's message and one of her most popular teachings and expanded it into this, her first book.

Meredith and her husband, Josh, have four children and two dogs and call College Station, Texas, home.

Connect with Meredith at MeredithPerryman.com.

Made in the USA
Middletown, DE
26 March 2024